# Fractured
*Living with Grief*

Carole L. Sanek

*Fractured.* Copyright 2020 by Carole L. Sanek. All rights reserved. No part of this publication may be reproduced, distributed, or transmitted in any form or by any means, including photocopying, recording, or other electronic or mechanical methods, without the prior written permission of the publisher, except in the case of brief quotations embodied in critical reviews and certain other noncommercial uses permitted by copyright law.

For permission requests, write to the publisher, addressed "Attention: Permissions Coordinator," 205 N. Michigan Avenue, Suite #810, Chicago, IL 60601. 13th & Joan books may be purchased for educational, business or sales promotional use. For information, please email the Sales Department at sales@13thandjoan.com.

Printed in the U. S. A.

First Printing, November 2020.

Library of Congress Cataloging-in-Publication Data has been applied for.

ISBN: 978-1-953156-17-4

For everyone, because there is no escaping the reality that grief is the price of love. May you find peace, wise council, and comfort within these pages. My wish is that my experiences will not only help you but enable you to guide others experiencing grief.

*Carole L. Sanek,*
*Certified Personal Life Coach*

"A beautifully written and moving memoir, a testament to love, and an informative guide to navigating grief, all combined in this one book. Very helpful, first-hand knowledge, for those who are bereaved contained within these pages."

Ashley H.

Carole L. Sanek has entwined her timeless love story into a tapestry of hope and healing in *Fractured: Living with Grief*. The love, passion and heartbreak spiral off the pages and pull you into Carole's heartfelt world: before Larry, during their marriage, and after Larry passes. In *Fractured: Living with Grief*, Sanek has woven her account of manifesting the man of her dreams, their story of an endless love, and her journey to heal and go on after her husband's untimely passing.

The author enchants the readers with her grandmother, encouraging her to *"fall in love with love."* After turbulent relationships and a thirty-year search for "a man who would care for me like no other;" Carole and Larry find each other. After a *"magical night when we both began to heal from our pasts and began to become whole, again,"* they had a whirlwind relationship and were married for twenty years of ecstasy.

The adventures and tender moments of their marriage are reminiscent of the bygone era of Paul Newman and Joanne Woodward. *Fractured: Living with Grief* is a true tale of love from their exhilarating trips to dancing in their lanai and through the rooms of their home. There are moments of laughter, but sadly their story snaps back to the reality of Larry's sudden passing. Carole L. Sanek clearly expresses, *"I find that grief is like being caught in a sudden undertow. It grabs you and pulls you down into* the black abyss of anguish with no warning, and swimming against the current is impossible."

The beautiful element interwoven is Sanek's realm of raw emotions she shares, while bringing hope and sharing guidance, advice and resources to help others feeling unbearable grief after suffering the trauma of loss. Her intimate journey from moments before Larry's collapse to the days in the hospital and the twenty months that follow include a range of feelings and responsibilities that Sanek outlines step-by-step to help the grief stricken. One important component included is advice of do's and do not's for the family and friends surrounding those in mourning. Carole L. Sanek stresses, "*I want everyone to remember that you are wonderful because you are living each day with pain that other people cannot even fathom. Read that again.*"

Professor Donnalynn Scillieri, M.A. 5 Stars

"Down-to-earth, warmhearted, feisty, frightening (to anyone who fears losing anyone they love, which is ALL of us) unexpectedly funny in the sharing of Carole and Larry's love story, and absolutely essential reading,".

Dot Cannon, host, Over Coffee® podcast.

My wife Paula and I first met Carole and Larry five years ago when we were both part of a podcasters group on a memorable cruise together. From the first time we met, the love that Carole and Larry had for each other was so clear. They affected us as a couple who, like Paula and I, appeared to be so inseparable that you thought of them as a single entity. That is how couples who are so much in love become; '*the two become as one.*'

The book was so well written, as I read through *"Fractured,"* I could not help but live through Carole's eyes during the ongoing months of agony and grief. I married Paula, my college sweetheart, over 41 years ago, and I experienced Carole's story of grief with tears streaming down my cheeks.

This first-person account of Carole's life during the subsequent months after Larry's death is superbly woven between the beautiful story of love (which was their life), applicable quotes, and very practical tips and advice covering all the issues you will face after such a tragic fracturing of a love story. Through her story, Carole shows how strong she is and how her resolve allowed her to continue through the devastation.

We may never understand this side of heaven, why God allows the fracturing of a love story as beautiful as Carole and Larry had. As Carole so eloquently writes, when our earthbound love story ends, you never will fully get over the grief, but you learn how to live with that grief, as difficult as that may be. I would not dare to offer platitudes on how to live a *"Fractured life."* At this point in my life is beyond my comprehension. I do know that Carole's gift to us in her book *"Fractured"* will help many who will, unfortunately, have to learn how to continue by *"Living with Grief."* Isaiah 55:8, *"My thoughts are nothing like your thoughts,"* says the Lord. *"And my ways are far beyond anything you can imagine."*

*"Fractured – Living with Grief"* is a must-read for everyone, but especially for those who are dealing with a love life that has been fractured through death. An outstanding 5-star book!

H. Guthrie Chamberlain, III, Podcaster,<br>Wisdom-Trek.com

What a feat! Carole has written a book that is both gut wrenchingly beautiful and equally helpful. *Fractured* is a book all who are grieving, or know someone who is, should read.

Jenna Edwards #1 best-selling author<br>and host of the Aggressive Optimism podcast

*Widowhood is learning to live fractured and knowing when pain is healing and when it is harmful.*

*Fractured* is a widow's walk through author Carole Sanek and late husband Larry's love story, his tragic death, and the pains of healing. She is a nurse and cares for people. He is an engineer who is focused and cannot be deterred from his projects. In this soul baring book, new widows may find their touch stone. When words often fail or are too often unspoken, Carole lends her authentic emotional thoughts, reactions, and responses. Carole writes her truth in the rawness of new grief and she does it well. She has a gift for writing and offers us healing through her writing. She draws her reader into her story through vignettes of the love, the shenanigans, the turmoil, and the achievements of her marriage. At the same time, she reconciles the stark irrational shock of becoming and being widowed.

Carole became a widow suddenly, if there is ever any other way. In the middle of dinner, Larry went to water the rose bushes, lost consciousness from a stroke, and died two weeks later.

Widowhood came to me in the middle of a fast-paced life as a working mother of two teenagers. This book is needed; I wish I had *Fractured* to read in my first year widowed because of the insurmountable, surreal thoughts that were foreign to me then.

These types of thoughts now seem to me to be universal to early widowhood. No matter where you are in the struggle to overcome grief, this book will aid in the discovery and understanding of a new widow's identity and the necessary reconciliation of deep sorrow together with the precious joys of life.

When you read *Fractured* you will see vibrant love and the struggles of a strong woman finding her way through grief to a new place of heightened awareness, independence, and strength. Larry loved Carole's bold moves and in a moment of anguish (or perhaps rage?) she decisively had the newly despised rose bushes taken away- an easy object to blame and remove.

Carole leads you through her journey, and at times, she tells you what to do. I laughed out loud when she writes "I cannot state this strongly enough. If you want invitations, you have to be bold enough to ask. If you have a yellow high-lighter, this is where you would use it."

If you miss reading *Fractured*, you will miss being cared for by a nurse and learning how she cares for herself. She wants to help you heal your fracture, as she is healing hers. Carole's realization and walk of the foreverness of love, loss, and longing of being genuinely loved comes with great vulnerability and immense pain. Her message resonates. She says Larry married a joyful woman and she seeks to rediscover her joy and to be the best of what he loved in her.

Carole includes a list of emotions and physical feelings that may accompany grief. If you find yourself asking if your emotions and physical feelings are normal or when do these feelings change or go away, then *Fractured* is a must read.

Megan Kopka,<br>
CERTIFIED FINANCIAL PLANNER™<br>
Widow, mother, and owner of Kopka Financial, LLC.

There are no roadmaps when walking the path of grief. As a minister, I have accompanied folk on this road. I have often wished for a guide to pass on to those grieving who can speak the language of the grieving process. Carole Sanek has done that with Fractured. She weaves her own story throughout the book with practical, helpful advice. One can feel her comfort, and love. This book is gripping and hopeful. Whether you are grieving or know someone who is, Carole's book is a gift.

Reverend Robin DeAngelis,<br>Groveland Congregational Church UCC, Massachusetts.

Author Carole Sanek's "Fractured: Living with Grief" is foremost, a beautifully written love story. In the telling, it encompasses dealing with tragic loss and navigating the aftermath of what she has aptly dubbed her own "Wilderness of Grief".

Into the telling of her story, she has seamlessly woven "guideposts" that offer precious, hard won information gleaned from her own experience. These guide posts provide a treasure trove of information to aid those who are currently navigating their own wilderness, to those wondering how to help someone who has recently experienced the loss of their "person", as well as practical guidance for those who must prepare for the impending loss of a loved one.

Ms. Sanek candidly relates her own struggles while gently offering suggestions for coping with the twists and turns of this oftentimes treacherous journey, including suggestions about when and how to reach out for professional help.

A particularly poignant and insightful chapter in Sanek's book is entitled "Slaying the 'Grief Dragon'" which begins:

"I often look at one of the many framed photos I have of Larry in my home, and I tell him this: 'Sweetheart, on 2/19/19 you laid down your sword. On 3/3/19 I picked it up in preparation of slaying the grief dragon.

I will never put grief in the ground, but I learned how I can have delightful days that outnumber the awful days. One day it just all changed, ever so slightly, but the change was welcome. As I journeyed through my wilderness, I saw flashes of sunlight appearing. I knew these glimmers were coming to me because I was reaching a new level in my grief. The pathway in my wilderness had started a gentle uphill climb. Sunlight was peeking through the cragginess of the large rocks."

In and of itself it is a spellbinding read, difficult to put down once started. It is a love story from beginning to end and like all good love stories, in the end, love triumphantly conquers all.

Sheila Polzin

I just finished Carole Sanek's beautiful book with grateful tears flowing. My tears were released by experiencing her deep love and life story. This is an emotional journey facing all of us. Sanek masterfully laid out the twists and turns, the pit stops and pitfalls to help us know what to expect for ourselves and others after a loss.

Sanek's ability to communicate all her emotions and all her humanness in 360 is what moved me in a world of sound bites and text communicating. She offers everything from practical tips to raw realities. She and her book are a gift to both my heart and my soul.

We have been friends for many years and worked together in business too, and I have to thank her for being my grief whisperer

- giving me and others an emotional roadmap and being our guide on this journey called "fractured" and how to lovingly find our way forward.

Cyndee Haydon, Realtor® in Tampa Bay, Florida<br>and author of "Secrets to Happy Home Selling".

And so it began……

*"I was falling. Falling through time and space and stars and sky and everything in between."*

Jess Rothenberg

December 11, 1998

# Contents

## Part One
The Very Beginning of Our Ending .................................................. 5

### CHAPTER 1
The Lights Went Out ........................................................................ 7

### CHAPTER 2
I Could Sleep, I Couldn't Eat ......................................................... 13

### CHAPTER 3
There Was No Going Back Now ................................................... 17

### CHAPTER 4
Fly High, My Love .......................................................................... 20

## Part 2
Pushing Forward ............................................................................. 25

### CHAPTER 5
There is No Loneliness that Compares to the Loneliness
of Grief ............................................................................................. 27

### CHAPTER 6
What is This Thing Called Grief ................................................... 32

**CHAPTER 7**
There is Nothing Normal in Any New Normal ........................... 37

**CHAPTER 8**
There is No Pause Button in Real Life ......................................... 40

**CHAPTER 9**
Crying Through Dinner ................................................................ 46

**CHAPTER 10**
When the Thunder Rolled ............................................................ 50

**CHAPTER 11**
Grief Rewrites Your Address Book ............................................... 54

**CHAPTER 12**
Choose Your Words Wisely, Now More than Ever Before ........ 59

**CHAPTER 13**
And the Grief Kept Coming .......................................................... 65

**CHAPTER 14**
Everyone Deserves a Goodbye ...................................................... 70

**CHAPTER 15**
The Anniversaries of the Heart ..................................................... 76

**CHAPTER 16**
There is No Rule Book .................................................................. 82

**CHAPTER 17**
Your Grief is not My Grief, It's All Yours ..................................... 87

**CHAPTER 18**
Slaying the Grief Dragon .................................................. 93

# *Part 3* ........................................ 99

**CHAPTER 19**
30 Years of Waiting.......................................................... 101

**CHAPTER 20**
Day 77............................................................................. 104

**CHAPTER 21**
Love Cannot Be Downsized ............................................ 111

**CHAPTER 22**
The Wisdom I Have Found in This ................................. 114

**CHAPTER 23**
Rock Steady..................................................................... 121

**CHAPTER 24**
#Superlove ...................................................................... 125

Chicago winters are nasty, and there I was sitting at my computer asking myself did I really accept a date for dinner with a man I had never met and walk three long blocks, freezing my fanny off? What was I thinking?

The truth is a good friend had convinced me to sign up for an online dating service, and I was down to my last few days of having free access to it, but free also meant I couldn't see any photos of the men there, nor could they see me. This truly was a blind date.

Doing this definitely took courage because either one of us could have been a dud, and then what? Yes, this took bravery along with a dose of what the hell was I thinking because it was freezing outside.

I primped. Who doesn't want to look terrific on a first date? Then again, who looks for a new relationship during the holidays? My brain kept telling me that the men on the site were probably trying to get lucky, I mean why else would they join at the holidays? It is like admitting they were bums that had gotten tossed out. Never mind the fact that I also had joined at the holidays.

I had returned to Chicago from living in Costa Rica with a stop in Detroit to visit friends before coming back to the windy city. On top of all of this, I was still married, although the divorce was imminent.

I primped some more. I won't lie, I went for a sexy look with a mini-skirt and low-cut top, and I added a spritz of "Obsession," my signature scent. I walked the three long blocks to the restaurant he had chosen in low-heeled shoes, still slipping and sliding along the way.

# FRACTURED

I walked into the restaurant, and the world stopped spinning for a minute. There he was, just as he had described, tall with a beautiful head of silver hair, and a look on his face that told me he appreciated what he was looking at, and in fact that look told me he felt as if he had won the lottery. I knew I had already won it.

It was a noisy Friday evening, people were laughing and talking, but all I could hear was the beat of my heart as I walked up to this amazingly sexy man. His smile lit up the room, and for the first time in a long time I was speechless.

We laughed through dinner; we told our stories, and suddenly the check arrived and all I could think was I had to come up with something to keep this evening going. I wasn't ready to say goodnight, and I had a feeling he felt the same way.

I suggested we take a walk over to Marshall Fields on State Street to look at the holiday windows without giving a thought to the fact that my skimpy attire was iffy for windy and blowy Chicago winter nights.

We were not that far from the restaurant when I realized I was having a wardrobe malfunction. I was wearing thigh-high nylon stockings, and they were slipping in the frosty weather. Undoubtedly this was because my thighs had shrunk from the cold, and it was all I could do to walk normally while occasionally trying to hike them back up.

I have always been a bold woman, and what I should have done was just stop and peel them off. But no, I continued to keep them where they belonged in the name of keeping this date going by doing some strange convoluted-looking dance.

Weeks later, when I admitted this to Larry, he laughed so hard his face turned red, and he came right out and asked why I hadn't just peeled them off without missing a beat. By this time, he had already learned how bold I could be, and the bolder I was, the harder he fell.

Yes, in looking back, that was the magical night when we both began to heal from our pasts and we both began to become whole again.

# Part One

## The Very Beginning of Our Ending

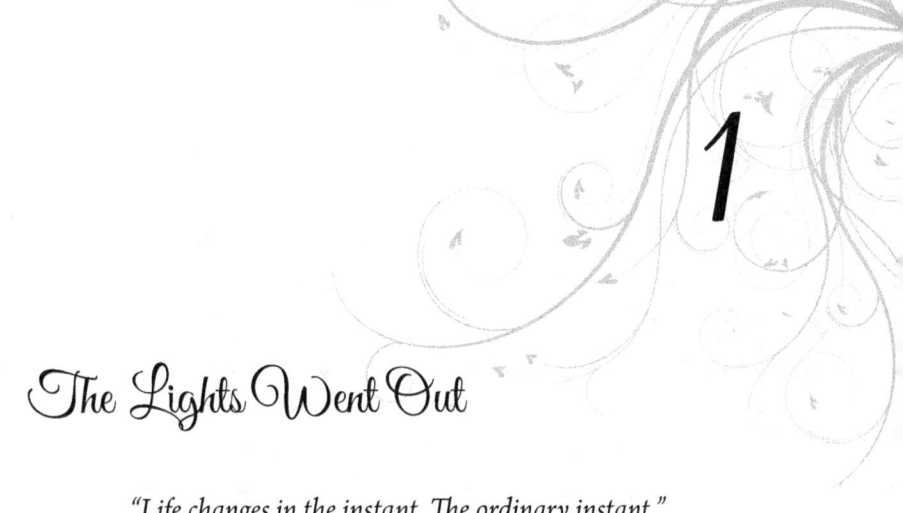

# The Lights Went Out

*"Life changes in the instant. The ordinary instant."*
Joan Didion

February 19, 2019 began like every other day in my life. I woke up about 90 minutes after Larry, and I walked out of our bedroom, saying my usual "Morning Renzo" to him. His smile would light up the room, and it turned into a hug and a kiss, morning breath and all. The dogs would be jumping and barking in excitement—this is how our mornings were for years. Then there was the coffee. It was waiting for me in my favorite mug, sweetened and creamed to perfection, and I would inhale the smell as I took my first sip. Little did I know that would be our last morning and that later that day everything would come to a screeching halt.

I was looking forward to getting dressed and hitting the road to go to the big box home improvement stores. We were finally getting ready to remodel the kitchen, and what woman doesn't want a spectacular kitchen? Maybe one who doesn't cook, but cooking was our date night. We cooked together almost every night of the week, and it was time to update the kitchen.

Larry had spent all day Sunday ripping out the existing backsplash and all the drywall down to the studs. He had removed all the cabinet doors in preparation of painting them, and I was ready to get this project started. In the 20+ years I had been with this man, I had been breathing construction dust annually because Larry was a DIY dude. I was his assistant, and the dogs were his superintendents.

It was a day like any other day. The sun was shining, the warm air was perfect, and his favorite country music was playing on the car radio. Normally I dislike going to these stores—I had spent a lot of time in them over the years. Larry was an engineer. If you have an engineer in your life, then you know when they put themselves into the project zone, there is no getting them out until they find everything they are looking for, and Larry was no exception. It took two stores to complete the shopping list, and we headed home for lunch with a car full of kitchen improvement treasures.

It was just another day in paradise, or so I thought.

Larry went to his office to work on some real estate ideas, and at about 4 PM he came out and told me he was feeling a little tired and he laid down for a brief nap. This wasn't unusual for him. He worked hard all weekend, and he was also the adult who got up with whining dogs in the middle of the night.

He napped, and I prepared dinner.

February is a beautiful weather month in Florida, and we ate outside on our lanai almost every evening. Tonight Larry took care of setting the table and pouring the wine while I carved the roast and plated our dinners.

As we finished eating, Larry remembered he had not fertilized the rose bushes that he'd bought and planted just for me, and he went out to do that. He turned and said, "When I am finished, I will come back in and have another glass of wine with you." Little did I know that those were the last words he would ever speak to me.

I sat there looking at the sunset and admiring the work Larry had recently done on the yard. I looked up as I heard the door open and watched Larry walk back into the lanai. He set the watering can down, turned and looked at me and said words that sounded like a foreign language. At first, I thought he was being his usual fun self, but then he tried to speak again, and I knew immediately he was having a stroke. There was no doubt in my mind.

I flew out of my chair and how I ever reached him across the back porch is a mystery to me, but I got to him, and I caught him and eased him into a chair.

He was unconscious immediately. I couldn't wake him. I tried a sternal rub; he had no response to pain, and that was the moment I knew that our lives had changed forever; he was in a deep state of unconsciousness.

I went into an extreme panic mode. I was running around looking for our bottle of regular aspirin to get one under his tongue; I had my cell phone in my hand and I was screaming into the phone at the 911 operator. I called my son, and I was screaming at him. I called Larry's daughter and I remember screaming at her saying her father was down. I called 911 again because it was past the time when they should have arrived. I was screaming and crying and swearing, and I felt as if I were dying too. I hit my knees with my cell phone in my hands, begging God to save this man. Then I saw the flashing lights, and within minutes Larry was on his way to the emergency room.

We all do odd things when we are in shock. I cleaned up the lanai of the food, the dishes, the wine glasses, and took everything into the house and put it away. I let the dogs out and I left for the hospital. I was a zombie.

# FRACTURED

I drove past the hospital entrance and had to backtrack. How I got there by myself I am not sure. I ran to the ER entrance, and they escorted me back. Larry was lying there with tubes everywhere. He had IVs running, they'd intubated him, he had a bladder catheter, and questions were being thrown at me from all sides.

I answered as best as I could while fielding phone calls from his adult children, my son, and a dear friend who worked at Tampa General Hospital. I asked our local hospital to transfer him there. Larry needed a hospital with an advanced primary stroke team.

The wait was agonizing. Someone put an iPad in front of me for a teleconference with a neurologist. A teleconference. The neurologist confirmed that there was in fact an infarct in his midbrain stem and told me a CT scan can not differentiate between a clot and a bleed. He needed more advanced testing.

I was in a daze. I was terrified. I knew this was bad; I had not spent years working in medicine as a nurse to believe this would really have a happy ending.

The ER doctor told me that Tampa General Hospital had accepted Larry, and a flight crew was on their way to take him there.

It seemed like hours, but as I looked at the clock it really wasn't; it is just that I knew that time was of the essence. I knew we only had several hours to get him help. I knew we were in a hospital that did not have a stroke intervention program, and that we were losing time.

The helicopter and flight crew arrived, and I signed the consent form to move him. I leaned over to him and said, "Well, Larry you never wanted to be in a helicopter, but we have no choice, so hang on tight. Hang in there, I love you with all my heart." I took his personal effects and left to drive to Tampa General Hospital.

Thankfully, I have friends who work there, and yes, I relied on these friendships. There was an advocate waiting for me in the ER. I went back to see him, and nothing had changed. Now we were waiting for the neurosurgery team to get there to take him to Interventional Radiology to remove the clot. He was still unresponsive, and I knew in my heart of hearts this was a terrible stroke.

Larry's daughter, Kristin, arrived with her partner, Simon, and finally the neurosurgeon came out to tell us that the clot was about the size of a small marble, and my heart sank even more. They located the clot in his basilar artery, where approximately only four percent of all strokes happen, and most strokes that occur there are devastating, if not deadly.

I had been praying non-stop. I didn't stop praying. I was bargaining with God. I couldn't cry. I was in shock. This could not be happening. We had such a love story; in fact, people talked about our love story. THIS COULD NOT BE HAPPENING. Yet it was, and we were all scared out of our minds, and I felt a deep pain in my chest as if a nail had been driven through my heart.

*"Change, like healing, takes time."*
Veronica Roth

February 11, 2019 was a day we had been waiting for because we would get the results of Larry's latest echocardiogram test.

Larry was two years out of a double coronary bypass, and his heart was never very happy after that surgery. During the operation it became apparent to the surgeon that something wasn't right with his hemodynamics (circulation of his blood). Upon further examination, he discovered the problem. Larry had an atrial-septal defect, which is a hole in the walls of his atria, the two upper chambers of the heart. The surgeon repaired the defect and Larry's heart but his heart had become accustomed to the defect over the years and had worked well with it. Now his heart was struggling to regain function, and Larry ended up being diagnosed with congestive heart failure while recovering from the surgery.

Over time, though, he was improving, and we were happy that his results were better, he still had congestive heart failure, but his heart was getting stronger. Larry let nothing stop him from living the way he always lived, in charge and pushing the envelope in working hard to get things done.

His cardiologist was happy with his progress, and we made an appointment for six months down the road, heaved a collective sigh of relief, and celebrated with a pleasant lunch at one of our favorite restaurants.

# 2

## I Could Sleep, I Couldn't Eat

*"I'm scared of the unknown future."*
Bethenny Frankel

Sleep was three hours long that first night, and when I woke, I got the dogs and all their supplies gathered together. I was taking a big chance that the kennel had space for them, as it was too early to call. It all worked out, and I sped down I-75 to the hospital. I had lived in Tampa for 14 years and still got lost down where the cruise ships dock. I did not think I would ever arrive at the hospital. It was déjà vu of the night before when I'd missed the entrance to the first hospital.

My GPS had failed me as did all my prior knowledge of where I wanted to go.

My memory had failed me also as the following days in the hospital seem to have blended together, and I could not remember what happened on what day. I know that my phone rang all the time with calls from friends and family.

I know I wasn't eating, and reality sank in that Larry probably could not come back to all of us this time. I knew it in my educational background; I felt it in my heart, and I saw it in the looks on the faces of all the doctors.

He tried, he really tried. We would all talk to him for hours to get just one slight glimmer of a response from him, and we could elicit small responses; however, most of the time he remained unconscious.

Over the weekend I had his RN put his side rail down and I crawled into bed with him and laid my head on his shoulder. I had his right arm around me and I chose our wedding dance songs. I put the phone next to his ear. As "Love of my Life" played by Sammy Kershaw, Larry moved his hand up to my head and caressed my curls. I knew he was with me then and was holding me tight. I also knew he couldn't get past all the damage to his brain and come back to me this time. Now as I look back at that day, I understand he was letting me know he couldn't do it. He tried so hard, he really did. The brain injury was just too serious. He was saying goodbye by loving me the only way he could—by holding me—and I wept in his arms.

I would drive back and forth to the hospital every day, 100 miles round trip, and the house was so lonely, so empty. The dogs were at the kennel, and I had a mess in my kitchen, no food in the refrigerator, and more sleepless nights.

As I ended the fourth day of this emotional and physical agony, I could only think of these words: "one day, one hour at a time."

## TINY BUBBLES IN LIFE

*"Her heart was made of liquid sunset."*
Virginia Woolf

It was the autumn of 1999, and we were sitting out on the patio of our condo sipping wine and talking about the upcoming winter in Indiana. I did not want to let go of warm weather. I looked at Larry and told him I had a lot of airline miles and hotel points, and we should use them before they expired at the end of the year. He looked at me and asked me where we could go. I had already picked our destination, and I asked, "How about Hawaii?"

It took Larry back, and he asked if I really had enough miles and points for both of us, and my answer was yes. I drove a hard bargain; he had to pick up all the food and fun and shopping, and I would handle the rest. Seemed fair to me, I thought. This is how we always rolled. Larry rarely said no.

We were off for eight nights in Honolulu, starting at Turtle Bay and finishing at Waikiki.

We landed at some ridiculous hour, exhausted. We picked up our rental car and drove up to Turtle Bay without luggage. It had not made the transfer of planes in Los Angeles, but we were so relieved to be there that it did not matter.

The next morning there was still no luggage, and we wanted to get into the pool and start our adventure; however, no luggage meant no bathing suits. No luggage meant we needed to head to the gift shop where the only bathing suits for women were barely there and I had to take a big gulp of air and just step out into the sunshine in the briefest bikini I had ever worn. I needed a lot of sunscreen, and Larry was very willing to apply it.

We would sit by the pool and relax with the drink of the day by our sides and smile at each other as we made plans to return. This was paradise.

We were so happy to be in Hawaii. It is so different from other beach areas in the United States, and we spent every day there immersing ourselves in the history and tradition of the islands.

We attended a luau. We rode horses on the beach. We drove to Waimea and hiked for hours, and then we shopped for beautiful souvenirs of our trip and met Moped Patty, who suggested a fabulous restaurant to celebrate our adventure on our last night before heading to Waikiki. Larry surprised me with a black pearl ring and a promise to return.

We were so in love; this was just a perfect time in our lives. We opened a bottle of Dom, and we laughed when the bubbles went up into our noses. We made love on the balcony of our hotel overlooking the ocean, arms and legs tangled in the bed sheets I insisted on wrapping ourselves in to hide from prying eyes.

This was a love story Hollywood makes movies about, and we never thought the champagne of life would go flat so quickly.

# 3

# There Was No Going Back Now

*"You never know how strong you are until being strong is the only choice you have."*
Bob Marley

Nine days had passed with no positive changes. Even though some physicians told us there was improvement, there really wasn't, and we as a family could see that. I was being pressed to sign for a tracheostomy and a feeding tube placement for transfer to a long-term care facility.

I discussed everything with his adult children, and we all agreed that Larry would never want extraordinary measures like that done to him. I had his living will with me, yet we held on, still hoping—and then there was no hope left.

I had searched Google, and sadly I got more defining information there regarding bilateral brain stem strokes to the basilar artery, and there was no encouraging news.

I asked to talk with the hospital psychologist; I asked to talk with the doctor who headed the palliative care team, and after those two discussions I gave my consent to honor Larry's wishes for no extraordinary measures. Respiratory Therapy came to remove him from the ventilator, and we moved him to hospice.

# FRACTURED

I cannot describe the emotional pain that falls upon anyone who has to abide by and honor the decision their person has made. It is a heartbreaking responsibility, and while it was so easy to sign those legal documents years earlier, it ripped my heart out of my chest to sign those papers that day.

We left him that afternoon in hospice, and when we got outside, it all hit me. It was then that I knew Larry would never feel the sunshine on his skin again, that he would never hear the birds sing, that he would never hold his dogs or hold me. It was all impossible, and I couldn't stop crying.

It was at this point that I experienced chest pain almost every day. I called it heartbreak pain, as it would happen right behind my breastbone, and I would rub it repeatedly trying to make the pain go away. It hurt so much.

I was alone now. Everyone who had been with me went to their homes. My loneliness level quadrupled as I walked into the house, and I knew eventually I would receive a phone call telling me Larry had died.

I posted on Facebook: "The love of my life, the man I took my vows with, the one I traveled the world with, laughed with, cried with, loved with was transferred today to hospice—we couldn't catch a miracle this time, but we had our share of them starting with the day we met and many more followed."

There was no going back now, and the pain was unbearable.

*"People love dogs. You can never go wrong adding a dog to the story."*
Jim Butcher

One Sunday morning I looked at Larry and told him I wanted a dog. You would have thought by the look on his face I was asking him for the world. I already had that, and I just wanted a dog. Our lives, our love for each other was so perfect I wanted to add to it and expand on our love. I wanted something to take care of because Larry was 98 percent perfect as he was.

Larry looked at me and asked, "Do you have any idea how much our lives will change with a dog?" I was standing there thinking to myself that he had forgotten that I had birthed and raised children. I know how children and puppies can change your life.

I won.

The search began. We visited pet stores; we answered ads in the paper, and one Sunday we drove out to the country, and after looking at four or five dogs, we still had not seen the one we wanted. We were about to give up when the owner brought one more dog out to meet us, and there he was, a perfect little light brown puppy with gray-tipped ears. We had our boy. We named him Taffy. We fell in love instantly.

Our lives were complete—or so we thought—and about a year later when we were at the pet supply store it changed again. There in a cage was the sweetest blond puppy boy up for adoption. He was only four months old, and he was already a rescue dog. We signed the papers immediately to adopt Corky.

Now our lives were more complete. Two dogs kept us busy, and I knew without a doubt that if anyone dared to mess with our boys that they would have to answer to Larry.

Our lives changed all right—for the better.

# 4

## Fly High, My Love

*"A butterfly always reminds that there is always beauty at the end of all the pain."*
Unknown

I went to bed on Sunday, March 3 with the intentions of spending Monday with Larry telling him over and over that it was okay to let go, that it was okay to leave me now, that I would be all right. The hospice physician told Larry's daughter that he thought Larry would live for several days, and I stayed home that day to allow her and our grandson to be with him.

I fell into bed emotionally exhausted and slept through the first phone call at 10PM. I woke at midnight to another phone call, this one telling me Larry had taken his last breath at 10:01. The nurses were in the room talking to him and caring for him when he died, and in looking back, I am so glad he was not alone.

I cannot describe how I felt. Again, it was surreal; this wasn't happening. I wanted to go back to sleep. I wanted to pretend this call had not come in, and that it was all a very bad dream, but I knew that wasn't possible.

I got up, got dressed, and drove to Tampa.

As I approached his room, there was a magnetic Monarch butterfly on his door to signify to all staff and any visitors that Larry had transitioned and to be cognizant of that and quiet in walking past the door.

I crawled into the bed with him and laid next to him and sobbed before kissing him one last time. I left the hospital and sat on a bench at 2AM holding that magnetic Monarch butterfly. I posted a photo of it and notified everyone on social media who had been supporting us and praying for us that the butterfly was on the door of his room when I arrived. Larry was at peace. My life had just turned upside down and inside out, and I had all this love in my heart with no place to go.

There definitely was no turning back, only moving forward, and I couldn't imagine even taking that first step.

I do not know how I drove home. I do not know how I did any of this on my own. As I look back all I can say is that it would only get worse over time because our lives and everything we did together in our businesses and in our personal lives had just changed, and no one prepares any of us for this change.

I had no clue what I would do now that my person had died.

*"Life is a gamble, so throw the dice."*
**Unknown**

# FRACTURED

Larry and I were conference junkies. I have lost count of all the conferences we had attended. We were both in real estate, and we attended many real estate conferences all over the country.

I was a content creator and writer for clients in social media, and we attended many conferences in that niche too.

Many were held in Las Vegas.

We could never say no to going there to have fun, eat great food, drink wonderful drinks, maybe learn something, attend shows—and oh yes, throw the dice at the craps table.

We were doing just that one afternoon, and Larry told this story many times afterwards. He finally realized that his stack of chips was going down in size because I was reaching under the table and helping myself to them. Oh yes, we always enjoyed our time in that city, and we had friends who live there, which made visiting even more appealing to us.

Larry could sit down at a poker machine and make $20 last an hour. We always had so much fun when we were in Las Vegas.

On one of our trips, we were at Caesar's Forum window shopping when his phone rang. He stood outside the entrance to the casino floor dealing with an offer of purchase on one of his listings, and I went in and $20 turned into $500. I always won more than Larry did in Las Vegas, because I was the bolder one in this marriage, and I took more risks knowing that everything would turn out just fine. He had a house under contract, I had dinner and show money.

We always enjoyed walking down the strip. We stopped to watch the elaborate shows many casinos put on at night. We would hold hands and stop to watch everything that was going on. We loved this crazy town.

We had a favorite bar/restaurant at the top of the Delano Hotel where we would sit and look down the strip at all the craziness below us and all those dazzling lights. Even in January when Las Vegas can be chilly, we would take our champagne glasses outside and just stare at the magnificence of it all. We were 64 floors up feeling as if we could touch the stars as we laughed and sipped champagne, always celebrating one more fantastic trip to Las Vegas.

We had both taken a big gamble on love and marriage, and it was worth any doubts we might have ever had.

# Part 2

## Pushing Forward

Part 2 is my guide, my gift to you and others about things that worked for me in my wilderness of grief. That's what I call the place where I spent most of my days, and grief calls me back to visit. As time went on, I emerged from the rocky crevices of pain more often, but in order for me to get to that place, there are things I learned I want to share with you.

# 5

# There is No Loneliness that Compares to the Loneliness of Grief

> *"I find that grief is like being caught in a sudden undertow. It grabs you and pulls you down into the black abyss of anguish with no warning, and swimming against the current is impossible."*
> Carole L. Sanek

I was alone in what was once our home. Our home had been lived in by two people head-over-heels in love. Now it was occupied by two dogs, one bird, and me, all missing Larry with every breath. No one prepares any of us for this. We see others who grieve; we know others who grieve, but when it is our turn, there is no game board to follow. No dice to throw, no wheel to spin to help us move along. Alone–learning to be alone hurts. It hurts like hell. You long for a person who can never return to you. THAT is the worst feeling of loneliness in the world.

There I was trying to survive a loss most people can't even imagine. No one knows how it feels until one day it happens and you are alone. There were times I looked and acted normal as if nothing had happened, and then I would remember my entire world had been swept away, and I was in free fall.

# FRACTURED

It stunned me; I was vulnerable, exhausted and weak. I couldn't move. I couldn't get dressed. I couldn't make coffee. I could hardly breathe.

I was physically ill. I was emotionally ill. It broke me.

I did not understand time, and all I could do was limp along as if I had suffered a broken leg that did not heal properly.

I wrote my daily thoughts, and as I re-read them, I can see how I just existed, I just went through the motions, I also wished at times that I had left this world with Larry. There was so much to do, so much to organize, and so much to agonize over.

I filled the first month with days where I looked for important paperwork. I had to file death certificates with many entities, including his life insurance company. I had to take a copy of his death certificate to the telephone company to get the account changed to my name. Things that should have been simple and easy took many phone calls and many tears.

I had only days to close a real estate business by state regulations. I had to go through banker box after banker box of contracts, taxes, receipts, and other legal documents. Larry had filled every nook and cranny, every shelf, every drawer in his desk with years of office supplies from previous businesses. He had six file cabinet drawers overflowing with correspondence from years before. He was a pack rat.

I realized that I couldn't possibly file income taxes in time, and this was the perfect time to hand things like that over to those who can help. Thankfully, a friend who is a CPA told me she would handle my extension and file our taxes at no cost to me and suggested I send a payment to the IRS to show good faith, and I did that.

Suggestion: Please accept the offers that friends make. Don't let pride stand in the way. You cannot do this all by yourself. It is hard enough to be alone emotionally at night. Let people help you.

I had a friend in California tell me he would handle all computer issues at no cost to me for as long as I needed him.

Our dog groomers offered free grooming for as long as I had the dogs.

Gift cards arrived so I could get take-out food.

Remember, if your person is on Social Security, that changes. If you are also on Social Security, that changes too. I had suddenly "lost" $1000 the first month, and I had bills.

Friends came to help me, and it surprised them to see all he had saved over the years. I cursed many times about this mess left for me to deal with, and that was only the beginning.

A friend and I packed up box after box of things we donated to schools, to charities, and took to shredding events. I spent every day going through things and organizing what to do with it all.

This was just his office; I couldn't even consider cleaning out the garage, which I had also asked him not to leave behind for me to deal with. I thanked Larry a lot in my head—and possibly out loud too.

It overwhelmed me. It will overwhelm you when/if this happens.

Confused was my middle name. Then thankfully, a friend whose husband also had passed away sent me a list of things I needed to take care of and how to do everything.

I did something I will be eternally grateful for in this new normal I now had. I reached out to hospice to meet with a bereavement counselor, and I credit this action with saving my sanity.

Please be aware of the fact that many hospice organizations offer free bereavement counseling, even if your person did not die in hospice care. They are there for those of us who grieve, and it is free help when we have no clue how our finances will filter out.

I learned so much, and I thought I had no space left in my brain to learn.

I learned that sometimes knowing too much is not a good thing at all.

I learned that I wasn't aware that I wasn't eating.

I learned that it was okay to ask for answers.

I learned that as much as I hate having to grieve, that it's often better to throw my arm around my grief and walk with it rather than trying to outrun it.

I learned the importance of stopping to say "I love you" even when you are so busy that the words don't want to come out of your mouth.

I learned how important it is to be aware of the value of every single moment.

I learned that I was not prepared to love someone so much that to no longer feel that love coming back to me brought me to my knees repeatedly.

*"The problem with heart disease is the first symptom is often fatal."*
Michael Phelps

It was in the early spring after we had gotten married, and I was getting breakfast ready. I heard Larry coming into the kitchen, and I turned to look at him, and his coloring was as gray as the gray shirt he had on that day. I looked closely at him and saw the beads of perspiration on his forehead. My stomach sank, and I asked him to sit down for a few minutes while I dashed into our bedroom to change out of my pajamas.

As I walked back into the kitchen, Larry asked, "I am not going to work today, am I?"

I told him we would take a detour to the ER, and that was the first time that I realized that this man I loved with all my heart could die of heart disease.

They admitted Larry for unspecified chest pain, and over the next several days he had several heart catheterizations and an angioplasty placing the newly approved drug-eluting stent in the artery cardiologists call the "Widow Maker." He was an instant celebrity and on the front page of the newspapers, and now he had to do what I had nagged him to do for quite a while—exercise. Only now it came in the form of cardiac rehab three times a week. I cracked the whip hard on this man. He would not leave me when we had just found each other. No way, no how.

# 6

# What is This Thing Called Grief

> *"Where you used to be, there is a hole in the world, which I find myself constantly walking around in the daytime and falling in at night. I miss you like hell."*
> Edna St. Vincent Millay

Grief is not your friend—or is it? I will explain that thought later in this book, because if you are newly bereaved and just starting on your journey, I want to prepare you for that thought.

Grief shows its ugly self in many different ways.

Emotionally, you may have these feelings:

- Sadness
- Anger
- Anxiety
- Numbness
- Shock
- Relief
- Isolation
- Guilt
- Helplessness
- Yearning
- Emptiness
- Loneliness
- Irritability
- Fear

Physically, you may feel:

- Hollowness in the stomach
- Shortness of breath
- Headaches
- Lack of energy
- Digestive upsets
- Tightness in the throat
- Oversensitivity to noise
- Weakness in the muscles
- Dry mouth
- Heart palpitations

Mentally, your thoughts may be filled with:

- Disbelief
- Forgetfulness
- Inability to focus
- Confusion
- Preoccupation
- Hallucinations
- Sense of presence
- Idealization of your loved one

Behaviors that you may have:

- Sleep—increased or decreased
- Social withdrawal
- Appetite—increased or decreased
- Frequent crying spells
- Lack of self-care
- Sighing

Spiritually you may feel:

- Pessimistic
- Loss of center
- Search for normalcy
- Lack of purpose

And there are probably other things I could add to these lists. Before you want to close this book and scream, remember these things are normal, and you won't feel every single one of them. That's a relief, right?

There is a difference between mourning and grief. Did you know that? Grief is the internal feelings and thoughts we have, while mourning is expressing it outside ourselves. It is important to mourn outside yourself. You need not be stoic; this is the time to tell people how you feel.

There is also no timeline in grieving. You own your grief. You own how you grieve. Please don't let anyone tell you where they think you should be in your journey.

Now let's move forward in reading this book and remember I wrote it with you in mind.

*"If there are no dogs in Heaven, then when I die I want to go where they went."*
Will Rogers

Our precious dog Taffy had medical issues that never got properly diagnosed. We had taken him to two local vets, and we finally took him to an emergency clinic.

Under anesthesia, the vets did a bronchoscopy and an echocardiogram. They told us that his lungs were fine, but he had chronic bronchitis.

This poor little dog coughed all the time. He couldn't stop.

He was on many medications, and sometimes he would stop coughing only to resume within hours.

We had a trip planned to go visit the kids and grandkids in Orlando, and we took all three dogs to their favorite kennel. We were only gone overnight, and when we stopped to get our dogs, the owner of the kennel said that Taffy had been coughing more than ever.

He was fine at home. Maybe he was just anxious about being away from Larry.

Taffy was Larry's little buddy. They were together all the time. Taffy slept on Larry's lap while Larry was working. They were best friends.

The next morning I had a work appointment and when I got home, I could see immediately Taffy was in trouble. Larry took him into the bathroom and turned the shower on to help with his breathing and coughing, but this didn't work. I put my foot down, and I made the decision that Larry could not make.

I called the vet and told them we were bringing our boy in, knowing he would not come home with us.

It was the worst of times for all of us. Taffy had been with us for 14 years, almost from the beginning of our marriage.

He laid on Larry's lap looking up at him, and we just sat there with tears rolling down our faces, knowing that we were doing the right thing, but dammit why did this have to happen to a sweet dog and a great family?

The vet took Taffy in the back to start an IV, and he was wrapped in a blanket and brought back to us to give us time to love him, to hold him, and to touch him as the vet administered the sedative and then the drug that took Taffy across the rainbow bridge.

# FRACTURED

My husband, the man who took no prisoners in business, the man who took down gang members fighting at his nightclub, the man whose voice when raised scared many people, that man collapsed with the agony of having his dog die in his arms. That man could not stop crying. That man couldn't get to his feet because he was grieving so deeply, and for the first time in our marriage I did not know what to do other than to hold him. That was my defining moment of the depth of the love I had for this man.

That was the real Larry. That was the man I gave my heart to knowing he would always take care of me. That was the man who loved the dog I wanted 14 years ago, and Larry never got over Taffy's death. We both cried when we looked at videos or photos of Taffy, and while the episodes of grieving this beautiful dog grew further apart, we both still cried five years later.

# There is Nothing Normal in Any New Normal

> "I didn't want normal until I didn't have it anymore."
> Maggie Stiefvater

On a good day I would like to take the person who coined the phrase "new normal" outside and scream at them about how nothing is f*cking normal in the wilderness of grief.

Everything changed, and nothing would ever give me back the normal I wanted. On a bad day I would probably flatten them.

How dare anyone try to tell me that what I was feeling was normal? My normal was waking up and walking out to the kitchen where Larry was handing me a cup of coffee every morning with a smile that could light up a room.

Now I woke to two dogs who needed to be fed, and no coffee cup being handed to me as I stumbled out to the kitchen. This was not normal.

How could it be normal to vacillate between a tsunami of tears or fits of rage and then calmly try to talk to many people on the phone to get answers to what they expected of me?

# FRACTURED

I would open the door to Larry's closet and stand there and inhale his scent. I would bury my head in his pillow. I would sit in his car just to capture his energy.

I dreaded every Tuesday night at 6:30PM, which was the time when he had his massive stroke. I couldn't even sit out on our lanai anymore because all I could see was Larry falling into my arms.

I couldn't break the habit of taking two of everything out at meals for quite a while.

No one prepares us for this, and how does one prepare? I had a friend tell me she knows if her husband dies first that she will leave Florida. I said nothing. I know there will be a lot of things she needs to do before she can even think about pulling up stakes.

"Everything I do is a love letter addressed to you."
Tayari Jones

January 1999, a month after we met, every morning began for me with coffee and an email from Larry. One would think in reading them we lived on opposite coasts and rarely saw each other.

We loved to express our feelings. Imagine this: Here was an engineer whose style of writing was always about dimensions and weight bearing and constructing high-rise buildings who was now writing love emails to a writer, of all people.

He wrote sweet emails, and then when desire hit him he would write steamy promises of our next night together.

I wrote back every morning, only my style of writing was more in the style of Elizabeth Barrett Browning and rarely in the style of E. E. Cummings.

Then one September morn, I wrote him my style of poetry about our love:

## YOU GIVE ME

*Passionate morning kisses before we get out of bed*
*2 minute voicemail messages just to say hello*
*Sly looks from across the room*
*Wisecracks that make me laugh out loud*
*Tender touches when no one is looking*
*The lingering scent of this morning's shower after you*
    *leave.*
*Gentle words meant only for my ears*
*Smiles that make me all warm and fuzzy*
*The peace that my chaotic world needs*
*Salty tears that fall on my cheeks*
*A cozy blanket on the coldest winter day*
*Answers to questions I have never asked*
*Strength and vulnerability all rolled into one*
*My safe place when things are bad.*
*My safe place when things are good.*
*You and I love you with all my heart*
*You and you are all I need.*
*9.4.99*

# 8

# There is No Pause Button in Real Life

*"And I pause for a while"*
Pink Floyd (San Tropez)

There is no rest for the wicked, so they say—well, there is no rest for the grieving either.

There was so much that I needed to do, and I was the only person who could handle it.

As I wrote, if/when you get offers of help, take them. If you get offers of anything that can lift some anguish from your heart, accept them.

In my grief wilderness I was alone for weeks, and everything fell on my shoulders. The weight of it all was already causing me to have neck spasms and pain behind my breastbone.

I needed a pause button, and there wasn't one for me to push.

I had to go to meet with the funeral director. How I drove to Tampa that day or how I sat through signing all the paperwork with his phone ringing off the hook is something I cannot remember. The funeral director's ringtone was the "Godfather Theme Song," and I wanted to rip his phone out of his hands every time it rang and smash it to the ground. He was a tasteless little man whom I needed, but I didn't need flashes of Don Corleone running through my mind while signing papers and paying for arrangements that would eventually bring Larry home to me.

The same week I had to meet with the funeral director I also had a dental emergency. This would be the first time I would walk into the dentist's office without Larry. My dentist was in Tampa, and Larry and I always went together. We would make a day of it, running errands, having breakfast or lunch, and shopping. When I told my dentist that Larry had just died, he walked me out of his office through the employee entrance and took me to my car. He did this so I wouldn't have to leave through the waiting room, look out, and realize that Larry wasn't sitting there.

- Suggestion: Be open with your doctor, your dentist, whoever. Speak up, use your strong voice to let them know you are grieving. They will help you.

By the end of this first week I received the phone call that Larry was ready to come home, and that is what I did: I brought him home.

I am resilient, but I would have moved heaven and earth to not have been alone.

- Suggestion: Don't do as I did. Take someone with you, especially at first, because people will tell you many things that you need to do and you will not remember these things later.

Here is a list I received from a friend, and while we live in Florida and this list was from an attorney in Florida, there are things on this list that will guide you in the right direction as you carve your path through your grief wilderness.

1. Order multiple certified death certificates. You need the short form and you will need the long form. The long form has the cause of death and life insurance companies and pension administrators will need this.
2. Check with your attorney if there is a will. Now is the time to make sure all legal documents are titled properly.
3. Have your home changed into your name.
4. File a certified death certificate with your county. Call them and ask who needs a copy because changes will need to be made.
5. If your state allows you to have a widow/widowers property value exemption, this office will also need a certified copy of the death certificate.
6. Contact your local Social Security office. The funeral director will do this, but you should do it too. Social Security has a minimal death benefit and will need a certified copy of the death certificate and a certified copy of your marriage certificate.
7. Change joint financial accounts, CDs, etc. at each bank and brokerage house to your name. One exception to this is keeping one joint account open for any checks that might come in your spouse's name.
8. In time you will need to have your own will, power of attorney, medical surrogate, and living will redone.
9. Cancel the deceased's debit card and destroy it.
10. File the life insurance claim. This includes any policies at their place of work.
11. Notify the deceased's former place of work if there is a pension, 401(k), stock options, etc.

12. If you still work, check with your employer about all that you take part in and change your beneficiaries.
13. Change your beneficiaries on your own life insurance policy, investment accounts, IRA, etc.
14. Change country club dues if you belong to one or anything else you both belong to.
15. Contact all companies you have joint insurance with and prepare to pay more as a woman.
16. Change the name on car titles, boats, etc. You will have to go in person to your tax collector's office. Call first and ask them what they need.
17. Change all reward accounts. This is something we don't think about. If you both belong to a frequent flyer club, you may be able to transfer their miles to your account. Call the airlines and ask.
18. Cancel any travel plans, tickets, etc. File for a refund with the appropriate vendor. Keep the deceased's credit card open if it was used to make the purchase.
19. Cancel the deceased's driver's license.
20. Cancel the credit cards once refunds have been processed.
21. Cancel the deceased's cell phone.
22. If you have unused amusement park tickets, call and ask about having the tickets re-issued to someone else in the family.
23. Cancel the deceased's voter registration card.
24. Federal income taxes for the year of death can be filed jointly.
25. Contact the VA if applicable for potential benefits.

26. In most cases, you are NOT responsible for debts in the deceased's name. I did not have to pay his credit card or his medical bills. I had to get tough and stand my ground, but they finally realized I was correct.

There is so much to go through, so much to handle, so many mind-boggling things. I made list after list, and I wasn't sure I would ever catch up.

As I went through things, I began to realize that I needed to get organized too. The last thing I ever would want to do to my family is leave them with things to go through. That would be too burdensome in this fast-paced world.

I stumbled upon a wonderful article written by Shoshana Berger and BJ Miller that was published online by Time Magazine. The title of it is "Why You Need to Make a 'When I Die' File—Before It's Too Late." It is a short and sweet guide to getting your shit together before you die to make it so much easier for your loved ones.

You may not feel like doing this right away, but please put it on your to-do list. Since that time I have made a will with designations, and I have made lists of who gets what. Be good to your family, because they are going to be good to you at your end.

"Every man dies – not every man really lives."
William Ross Wallace

Larry lived. Just like the Sinatra song "My Way," he lived. He did it his way too. He could be a stubborn son-of-a-gun, or a pussy cat depending on how an idea was presented to him.

We were getting ready to sell our home in Indiana and move to Florida. It was a two-bedroom home with a bonus room. Our agent suggested putting a closet in it to call it a three-bedroom home, and Larry went right to work. He stopped doing everything else and built that closet.

When we ripped the carpeting out of our Florida home and replaced it with tile, he went to work for several weeks straight until it was done. He was a hard-working, stubborn man who did things his way. I could hear that wet saw in my sleep. Oh wait, Larry is probably still cutting tile.

His actions aggravated his family at times; however, Larry's brain was wired to get the project done, period, end of story. I think back as I write about how unimportant it was for any of us to get our shorts in a wad over Larry's decisions.

Yes, he lived, and he really loved. He loved his family fiercely, but he took no prisoners. He truly was all about doing things his way. I learned to duck and hide over trying to change his mind.

There is no temper like that of a 6'2" Polish man, and I had seen that side of him in business, at people who ticked him off, at other drivers, you get the picture.

"My Way" was his theme song.

# Crying Through Dinner

> *"And there are days that I know why the Weeping Willows Weep..."*
> Maria Koszler

I was about three weeks into this unknown life, and cooking was the furthest thing from my mind. Larry and I cooked together every night. He was my sous chef, and he loved helping me. He also loved eating everything I prepared. He was almost a perfect husband.

I was living on tasteless frozen dinners, and I finally put it on social media that I needed food. What came to me were gift cards, and while I appreciated those, I really was hoping someone would pick up the baton and order a meal delivery service for me for several months.

- Suggestion: Ask for what you want.

A dear friend showed up with containers of food, and it relieved me because I didn't have to think about dinner for a while, and I could concentrate on other areas in my life.

Eventually I did some cooking. I was tired of frozen dinners, and I had eaten all the food my friend brought me.

The first meal I made was one of Larry's favorite meals, beef stroganoff. I set my plate down on the kitchen counter, sat on a barstool, and tried to eat that meal. I picked up my fork, and I cried. I couldn't stop the tears from falling. From that day forward, I often cried at dinner. My heart hurt so badly for a long time I couldn't eat dinner without tears.

I could not eat dinner out on our lanai or at our dining room table. That was impossible. So every night I ate dinner at the kitchen counter, and every night I cried. I lost weight. In fact, I lost 25 pounds.

One morning I reached into the pantry for a box of cereal and realized this would be the last bowl poured from that box. That box was Larry's cereal. He'd bought it; he'd brought it home. He'd opened it, and he'd habitually poured himself a bowl every morning except for bacon and eggs Sundays.

And I cried.

Now that more time has passed, I will share that I cried through my Christmas dinner too and I threw it away. I could not eat at our dining room table, and I did not cook as I used to cook. I call what I was doing cooking to eat.

I know that I am not the only widow/widower whose eating and cooking habits have changed. I occasionally order take-out from a favorite Thai restaurant, and I get several meals out of one order.

- Suggestion: Order take-out or order from a restaurant that delivers.

Who says you HAVE to cook? You don't. I still don't do it often. I try to make bigger meals that I can freeze and have later, and I make a lot of soups.

If you search online, you will find many recipes for one serving. It is so difficult to stop cooking enormous meals. I totally understand that after 20 years of preparing them.

As I wrote earlier, we prepped almost every meal together. On Saturday afternoon, if we had no plans to eat out we opened a good bottle of wine, and we would create a culinary masterpiece. Weather permitting, we would dine outside with candles, and music, and the dogs.

When dinner was over, we would dance, and we loved to hold each other and barely move.

I miss those moments. They were special, private, and we usually brought them to a close by falling into each other's arms in bed.

Cooking is a vast part of a relationship, and yes, you have food options. Be bold, try them. You need to eat. You need your strength.

Eat, just don't overdo it.

Larry would be the first person to tell me to stop crying through dinner, and I can hear him say "Hey, Carole, remember when I…"

Since that time, I am now finally able to sit at the table and eat without crying. It took a while, but I finally arrived. However, it also took moving twice and leaving some very sad memories hundreds of miles away.

*Laugh loudly, laugh often, and most important, laugh at yourself.*

Chelsea Handler

Larry had no problem laughing at himself. He had no problem looking silly. He sprayed his beautiful silver hair pink for a breast cancer fundraiser. He rode that crazy bull they came to your table with at a popular steak house on your birthday, and anywhere hats were sold he would put one on his head, and I would take pictures. He was so cute wearing a pink flamingo hat.

We always seemed to travel on Larry's birthday, and 2018 was no exception. I had always wanted to go to New Orleans, so we went. Goodness, we had a wonderful trip eating and drinking ourselves through that city. Then there were the beignets.

On his birthday we had lunch reservations at Commander's Palace, and I had let them know it was his birthday. They made a big deal of it, and soon Larry was sporting a tall chef's hat and all the servers, serenaded him, and he looked silly, but he loved it, and I loved him for it.

There were so many times when his actions landed him on my Facebook page. He would always look at me and ask if I was going to tell the world, and I would just look at him.

He never minded because he knew his antics made others laugh, and Larry's goal was making people laugh every day. And he succeeded.

"Laissez les bon temps rouler." We did.

# 10

## When the Thunder Rolled

*"Life has to end, love doesn't."*
Mitch Albom

The thunder began to first roll for me when I realized how much physical work I had to do. It rumbled around inside me, and I felt like an over-filled balloon ready to burst. It pissed me off.

There were so many things that made me angry, starting with all the work that Larry always promised me he would do and never did. Throw in the fact we never made plans for when this day arrived. I was very angry that he had left me—and he left me with all this shit to clean up and handle.

It angered me that everything I believed wouldn't happen for years yet had changed.

I could go on and on; however, I think you get the picture.

Then there was my anger at God. Oh, goodness, I was so angry at Him. I had waited years for someone to love me and accept me as Larry had, and it wasn't fair that God took him from me so soon.

It wasn't until I took a trip to a special spa in New Mexico where I took part in many types of therapies that I forgave them both.

I didn't really want to harbor anger at Larry or God, but anger is a part of grief.

Who wouldn't be angry? Anger can be healthy and it can also be unhealthy. We want to blame someone; we need to blame someone.

Anger sneaks up on us when memories come to mind, and we realize that there are no more memories that we will make.

There is also appropriate anger, and we may all have exhibited this form of anger from time to time.

- We take a tennis racket and beat the bed with it.
- Or maybe we have a peaceful place where we can speak our anger out loud.
- Writing. That is what I did. I expressed my anger in my writing.
- Physical activity: walk, run, work out, just move.
- Seek some counseling.

Be angry, but let go of the anger. Larry did not want to leave, and neither did the person you love want to leave. Work on it, and if you need help, ask for it.

Anger will ebb and flow, though. Over the months, I felt other furious moments.

Remember this: well-being is very important. Your well-being, my well-being—this matters.

Do what you need to do for peace in your heart and your head and your gut. I feel many times we get stuck because we don't erase things from our lives, and we allow these things to take bites out of us. We prefer to bleed over moving forward and away from the familiar, even when the familiar is painful.

I will always champion getting help. Help doesn't have to cost a fortune either. My grief therapist is free to me through hospice, and while Larry died in hospice care, they are there to counsel all who grieve. Check with your local hospice organizations.

If you have insurance, check to see what they will cover if free therapy isn't available to you.

If you live near a university, check to see if they are offering any counseling through studies they may be doing. I found one near my home, and it has been the best therapy I could have received.

If you dislike the first person you share your thoughts with, change. They work for you. It is not the other way around.

Many organizations and individual therapists offer free or affordable counseling.

- Insurance Parity and Affordable Counseling
- Crisis Care Hotlines
- Free Treatment for Mental Health Emergencies
- Sliding-Scale Affordable Therapy
- College and University Counseling Centers
- Therapists and Counselors in Training

You deserve to treat yourself well, and yes, that might mean asking for help.

*"I have been driven many times upon my knees by the overwhelming conviction that I had nowhere else to go. My own wisdom and that of all about me seemed insufficient for that day."*
Abraham Lincoln

It was eerily quiet one early morning. There were no breath sounds coming from the other side of the bed, and as my eyes grew accustomed to the dark I realized I was alone.

I got up and quietly opened our bedroom door, expecting to see Larry sleeping in the recliner which he sometimes did, but he wasn't there.

I tiptoed down the hallway, and in the stillness of his office with only the light of his computer monitor, I could see him on his knees praying, with tears streaming down his face.

I froze in place. This was a very private moment for him, and I was thinking about how I could retreat with him knowing I was there, but I failed. He looked at me, I looked at him, and he burst into tears, telling me he was terrified of his upcoming heart surgery. He was praying to God to bring him through it for me, for his family, for our future. I fell to my knees and prayed with him, the Catholic boy, the Protestant girl locked in an embrace, both crying out of fear.

After Larry had his surgery, they gave him a small pillow in the shape of a heart made by a group of women from a local church. The pillow is to be used to cushion the incision when a patient has to cough or sneeze and also to wear between the seatbelt and a patient's surgical wound.

That pillow has traveled with me; it has gone to my private yoga/energy class with me. It sits next to me in my car. I talk to it; I hold it; I cry into it. This pillow carries Larry's energy, and I look at it and see Larry wearing it the first time he could drive after surgery.

That pillow is filled with love. Love from the woman who made it, love from Larry, and love from me, because it is always close to me.

# 11

# Grief Rewrites Your Address Book

> *In the end, we will remember not the words of our enemies, but the silence of our friends.*
> Martin Luther King, Jr.

I really pondered that MLK, Jr. quote because I have exceptional friends still with me, still calling me, still supporting me, and they are loyal to me to this day. You all know in life, though, that we know and have disloyal people in our lives.

When Larry died, my phone rang a lot, text messages came in, and cards arrived in the mail—gifts too.

Then things slowed down, and a lot of communication stopped. I had so many should-a, would-a, could-a comments given to me that never happened. I know now that these things might have happened if I had pushed for them to happen; however, I was not in an emotional place to do this.

More time went by, and soon all communication dwindled down to the special loyal friends who have never stopped reaching out, and for that I am deeply grateful.

I am a bold person, though, and I reach out; I ask friends to have coffee, to meet for wine, to have lunch or dinner, and no one has failed me by saying no.

I cannot state this strongly enough. **If you want invitations, you have to be bold enough to ask.** If you have a yellow highlighter, this is where you would use it.

I also found that this is an excellent time to make new friendships because you really do not have to tell your entire story. You can just say you are widowed and move forward.

You will feel abandoned. I belong to grief groups on social media, and loneliness is a common thread that gets written about all the time.

If anyone has heard of Alan Wolfelt, PhD, then you know that he is one of the biggest experts in bereavement and grief. His website is https://www.centerforloss.com/, and I highly recommend visiting it and reading the wonderful articles he has written.

Dr. Wolfelt has written about how people will fall into one of three groups in your grief. This is what he wrote in his article "Reaching Out for Help when You are Grieving." I borrowed his rule of thirds from this article.

Dr. Wolfelt wrote:

> *In my own grief journeys and in the lives of the mourners I have been privileged to counsel, I have discovered that in general, you can take all the people in your life and divide them into thirds when it comes to grief support.*
>
> *One third of the people in your life will turn out to be truly empathetic helpers. They will have a desire to understand you and your unique thoughts and feelings about the death. They will demonstrate a willingness to be taught by you and a recognition that you are the expert of your experience, not them. They will be willing to be involved in*

*your pain and suffering without feeling the need to take it away from you. They will believe in your capacity to heal.*

*Another third of the people in your life will turn out to be neutral in response to your grief. They will neither help nor hinder you in your journey.*

*And the final third of people in your life will turn out to be harmful to you in your efforts to mourn and heal. While they are usually not setting out intentionally to harm you, they will judge you, they will try to take your grief away from you, and they will pull you off the path to healing.*

*Seek out your friends and family members who fall into the first group. They will be your confidants and momentum-givers on your journey. When you are actively mourning, try to avoid the last group, for they will trip you up and cause you to fall.*

I bounce back and forth between one and two, but that last group I call "okay then," and in this group are people who have hurt me deeply, embarrassed me (in public), yelled at me on social media, made inappropriate sexual remarks to me,, and they are unfriended, blocked, and gone.

Whenever someone crosses the line, I say to myself, "Okay then, you are gone." Some won't even cross the line; they just disappear, and I shrug my shoulders and move forward.

Face it, your life has transformed. This means you will lose friends and that you will also find out who your genuine friends are.

I will say this one more time: **If you want to be included in things, you have to be bold enough to ask.**

Start small, maybe with a coffee meetup, then move on to lunch, or even late afternoon lunch. Go shopping with a friend, go to a museum, go to a movie, go for a walk. There are so many things you can do. Me, I avoid dinner out with couples. That is painful.

Join an exercise group. Take a yoga class. Smile at the new people you see, let them know you are friendly.

Make new friends, but keep the old. Remember that little round that we sang in school? I have found that new friends have helped me a lot.

Doing all this has helped me move forward, and I knew writing a book could help others.

*"I had no friends. I wasn't there to make friends.
I was there to win."*
Ted Lindsay

Larry was very friendly; however, he had no friends. I never understood this. We could be out in public and former employees of his would be so happy to see him. They always said he was the best boss they ever had.

We were in Nashville, the bellman was coming with our luggage, and he looked at Larry and said, "Larry, I worked for you in your nightclub." Again, he extolled Larry's virtues as a boss.

I would ask him and he would tell me he always worked so hard and so long that he didn't have room for friends, AND he also shied away from having friends in the workplace.

# FRACTURED

I know he had a group he hung around with in college. I assume he had friends when he ran the Babe Ruth league. I also know he lost a friend in a motorcycle accident.

He was an amazing friend to me; he liked most of my friends; he liked being with other people, but he had no friends.

I made him promise that if I jumped off this earth first that he would move closer to his daughter because I knew he wouldn't be strong enough to live without human contact just like I knew I was the emotionally stronger partner in our union.

I guess I was the only friend he wanted, and I did not let him down. Friendship is about trust. I could write chapters on friends who break the trust in a relationship, lesson learned.

We were best friends.

# 12

# Choose Your Words Wisely, Now More than Ever Before

> *"Sometimes you just don't know what to say."*
> Laurie Hernandez

I could write volumes about all the things people should never say to anyone at many different times of their lives. It happens to all of us.

Now that I think about it, I have written volumes over the years about what to say to people who have been diagnosed with cancer (or any devastating disease), and I have always found it comes down to this: When you don't know what to say, give a hug.

I am one of those people, the ones with a cancer diagnosis, and I can remember the things people should never have said, but I also remember those who said the right things.

One of the best things you can say to anyone who is going through the worst days of their lives is to ask a question.

- What do you need?
- What can I do for you?

- I am going grocery shopping. Can I pick something up for you?
- Do you need me to go with you to…..?
- Can I pick the children up for you?
- Would you like me to just sit with you?

Do you see how these questions are all said with kindness? When we are grieving, we need kindness.

Yes, people will often say no. Don't push them to say yes. Also, please look us in the eyes when you ask a question, and if you are a close friend, take our hands.

On the flip side, there are many things you should never say. Let me share my thoughts on this:

- *He/she is in a better place.* No, they are not. If possible, their better place would be here, and they would be well again.
- *He/she is no longer in pain.* Do you really think this is a wonderful thing to say to someone?
- *You'll get married again.* (I had this said to me twice the day after Larry died.)
- *It's time for you to move on.* (We don't move on, we move forward.)
- *I am sure it will all be better soon.* How would you know? You don't live inside their thoughts and feelings.
- *God's plans are always the best, I am sure He has something better in store for you.* Oh, goodness, this is a terrible thing to say.

Again, close your mouth. Give a hug instead.

There will also be times when a remembrance day happens. Most friends don't know your wedding anniversary date, they probably don't know your spouse's birthday, and the same goes for the day your spouse died.

In my world because I am very transparent, most of my friends know the days that will knock me to my knees and leave me in a puddle of tears.

I also remind people, or maybe I am warning people a certain day is coming. Actually, I let people know because I need phone calls; I need people to reach out and touch me.

Our loved ones lived. They still live in our hearts. They deserve to be talked about and remembered. I cannot stop advising how much kindness counts on these days.

- Send a card
- Send flowers
- Ask to visit
- Bring wine
- Bring coffee
- Bring food
- Give them a big meaningful hug

We want to know you honor us, and we want to know you honor them.

Acknowledge their/our pain. You cannot take it away, just acknowledge it. Let them know you are there for them and that you will listen. Listen often and leave the advice at home. Above all, be able to be comfortable with difficult emotions. Let them talk. Let us talk.

I spend a lot of time in grief groups, and the chief complaint I read about are the people (family members) who tell a grieving person to get over it. I have a friend whose children stopped talking to her after her significant other died.

# FRACTURED

People mean well, I get that; however, I cannot say strongly enough that many times a hug is better, bringing a meal is even better than that, and choosing your words before you say them is the best thing you can do.

At the very beginning of my grief, I had a visit from a friend who spends a lot of her time working in the world of emotional intelligence. We had a long talk about this topic, which sent me to doing more research on it than I had ever considered.

The most emotionally intelligent people know that besides understanding their own emotions, it's important to perceive the emotions of others, and how their environment affects those emotions.

Somehow in grief, people stumble. They let us down, and we eventually forgive them when we share our grief with others who are also grieving.

I was at a meeting one day at a hospital where the discussion centered on the fact that many doctors lack emotional intelligence. They can talk about medicine and science, but many cannot talk about understanding emotional feelings.

I found the best site that described what the signs of low emotional intelligence are and you can find these signs here:

- https://www.verywellmind.com/signs-of-low-emotional-intelligence-2795958

Lack of empathy stood out. We all know people who just do not understand our pain and never will.

I move forward from these people. I let them go. I had to for my own well-being. I know it is difficult to let go; however, how many times do you want a kick in the gut to happen to you?

Larry died. I didn't get angry and break up with him, or file for divorce. I am not minimizing the pain that goes with those decisions; however, there is a huge emotional difference between a breakup or a divorce vs a death.

*"It is not how much you do, but how much love you put in the doing."*
Mother Teresa

Larry was not a saint—who is? I wouldn't want to paint him as a perfect person because none of us are perfect. No, he had his faults, and one of them was his engineering brain that didn't allow him to think outside of it.

When we were first dating, his daughter said to me, "Wait until he is working on a project—you will not be able to distract him from it." She was right.

About ten years into our marriage, I chose to have an elective surgical procedure done right around the Thanksgiving holiday.

I was instructed to stay in bed as much as possible for 3-4 days, and I was good with this. I had turkey leftovers in the refrigerator, my nightstand was set up with my pills, beverages, and the TV remote, and I had my laptop.

What I didn't have was a caregiver. If Larry were here today, he would admit he isn't a caregiver. He can't hover; he has to work on something.

Thankfully, I could text him on my phone to bring me a meal. The problem with meals was I don't like turkey leftovers, and this was the Monday after Thanksgiving—by now it was dried out and just not appetizing.

I muddled through and I didn't complain (then), but I let him know my feelings weeks to months later, probably once a week. He took it like a champ.

He put the love in helping me as much as he could. The bottom line is he was always there for me, and I married him knowing he couldn't cook, so dried turkey it was, and I ate as much as I could.

Then there was the day that I drove his beloved Durango to a friend's house and ended up rear-ending another car. I was in quite a state of nervousness calling him on the golf course.

I told him I was in an accident with his beloved Durango, and the first words out of his mouth were, "Are you okay?"

Smart man, kind man, loving man.

# 13

## And the Grief Kept Coming

> "Ask the animals, and they will teach you. Or the birds in the sky, and they will tell you. Or speak to the earth, and it will teach you. Or let the fish in the sea inform you. Which of all these does not know that the hand of the Lord has done this? In His hand is the life of every creature and the breath of all mankind."
> Job 12: 7-10

We had many pets in the years we were together. We started with our boy, Taffy, and then we added Corky to the mix, and Corky favored me over Larry until we brought Willie home. Three dogs ruled our home, and we wouldn't have had it any other way.

I brought the birds into our lives. Hop-Sing was my yellow cockatiel, and we added Pin, Piper, and Einstein over the years.

At a holiday dinner, a friend told us about a conure that needed a home, and we drove to northern Michigan to bring him home in the middle of winter because those of us who are rescued are those who rescue almost anything that breathes.

We had a houseful.

# FRACTURED

What none of us think about when we bring any pet home is that one day we will also let them go, and that the love they give us is short in time.

First Hop-Sing passed away, then Piper.

In the summer of 2014, Taffy crossed the rainbow bridge.

In February, just before Larry had his stroke, Pin took ill, and our bird vet told us he had kidney failure. We took him home. I kept him warm in a hand towel on my chest, and he passed away being loved.

When Larry was in the Neuro ICU, I received permission to bring Corky and Willie to see if their presence would get a response from Larry. Much to our surprise, Corky, who adored Larry, would not go near him on the bed. Willie crawled up into his arms and slept, but Corky couldn't, and as I look back now I realize that Corky knew his Larry was gone. He couldn't handle it.

I tried one more time when Larry was in hospice, and Corky would not go near him. Willie did; she tried to wake him up. Corky was so upset he threw up his breakfast. The Larry he loved was gone.

One beautiful sunny March afternoon I had fed the dogs, and I took them outside to sniff around and do their thing. Corky loved to sit in sunny spots, and he curled up in the sunshine while Willie looked for squirrels. Larry and I always allowed them to spend as much time as they wanted to spend outside. Willie signalled she was ready to go in, and as I opened the door, I saw Corky try to get up and he stumbled and fell over. He was confused and did not know which way to go.

My heart sank to my feet. I went to get him, and he was completely disoriented. I helped him into the house, and he laid down in the middle of my kitchen floor, curled up in a ball, and shook like a leaf.

That is when I knew this was all falling on me again, and that it was up to me to help him be with Larry. He was 17, and he was in good health. He was just old. However, I realized he was grieving. He had never been the same since the night that his loving friend was taken away by ambulance, and he just wanted to be with him.

At 6:30PM, yes at 6:30PM (again) on that Saturday I called our vet, and she agreed to come to her office and help Corky transition.

I called a friend to come stay with Willie, and I took Corky for our last car ride together.

I couldn't believe this was happening again, and so soon after Larry died. I could barely drive with all the tears I had in my eyes, and my heart was breaking.

This beautiful boy who had brought us so much love now depended on me to let him go.

I was exhausted and grieving and alone.

In June, that sweet conure we rescued let me know his time had come too, and after a visit to the emergency pet clinic, they informed me he had kidney failure and he flew high to be with those he loved to squawk at and torture. Einstein was very fond of Larry and undoubtedly is sitting on Larry's shoulder making Taffy and Corky very nervous.

Yes, I had tremendous loss within a four-month timeframe. I wouldn't wish this on anyone, and to this day I do not know how I did it, how I managed, how I got through it all. I kept asking why this was happening and all at once. What had I done in my life to deserve this? I know now that it was just their time. I got through it because I am so transparent in my life that I swear people can look straight through me. I wrote, they answered. Thank God.

# FRACTURED

Late summer of 2020 as I was getting ready to move from Florida, and the abundance of sad memories that surrounded me, when Willie took very ill.

She woke from a nap at her usual feeding time, and I watched her pace in circles holding her head to one side. I tried to pick her up, and she snapped at me as if she didn't know me. I called our vet.

We decided to watch her through the night. I did not sleep, she paced the house all night. I called the vet again and told her I was bringing Willie in, and I knew then, I would be coming home alone.

Lab work showed what the vet suspected. Willie had serious liver failure, and had become encephalopathic from the build-up of toxins in the bloodstream.

I held her for a long time as our vet helped her transition; there I was all alone, and for good now. I was in tremendous emotional pain.

Willie was my anchor to Larry. She was my faithful friend and companion. She loved me unconditionally, and now every fiber of my body and my brain that had entered the stage of accepting Larry's death, was torn apart. The chest pain returned, looking back, I am not sure how I remained standing after she died.

She was supposed to leave Florida with me. We were going to start new adventures, and write a new book about those adventures. Now, every possibility of that was gone.

"What the hell is this? The attack of the Planet of the Apes?"
Jason Medina

The cacophony of barking and squawking reaching my ears told me that something very wrong was happening out on the lanai.

Larry was in his office with the door closed recording a podcast and did not hear a thing. I went flying outside with my heart in my throat because I knew without looking that Einstein had gotten out of his cage. Willie, who is afraid of nothing, was barking at him as he flew around.

The lanai was screened, and Einstein couldn't sense the screening and flew into it. He bounced back and landed on the floor. That was what Willie was waiting for. She dived on top of him, and came up with the bird in her mouth.

The game began.

She ran around the lanai so proud of herself that she had finally caught the enemy. I couldn't catch her either. I was yelling at her to drop poor Einstein. She ignored me.

I finally cornered her, took my flip-flop off, and spanked her bottom until she turned and opened her mouth, which allowed Einstein to fall out.

I grabbed her and put her in the house, and then I checked Einstein for any signs of bite wounds. He was fine—scared, but fine.

That is when Larry opened the sliding door and asked why Willie was inside if I was outside. I just shook my head.

I told him the story, and he just laughed while my heartbeat slowed down and relief flooded over me.

Three dogs, three birds, and never a dull moment, except while everyone slept.

# 14

## Everyone Deserves a Goodbye

> "I didn't want to kiss you goodbye, that was the trouble;
> I wanted to kiss you goodnight.
> And there's a lot of difference."
> Ernest Hemingway

Larry died, and I felt old.

We never had that talk about what to do. In all the writing I have done since Larry died, many people have told me that as a couple they have made wills, they have made advanced directives; they have put all their passwords in a place in their home where they can be found.

We had all that, but we never had the emotional talk that went along with all this. Life is not a movie on the Hallmark channel. In fact, in this life, in the Game of this Life, there isn't a landing space that reads, "Your partner died, now you have to deal with all the shit."

I suddenly had a new identity. I was no longer Larry's wife. Pieces and parts of me died too. Nothing was comfortable. I doubted everything I thought about doing. Troubles cropped up like weeds in a garden, and I had to yank those weeds on my own.

At first other couples would invite me to join them for dinner. I did this several times until I couldn't anymore. Sitting around a table with married couples is not something I would recommend doing ever. If you can avoid it, do that.

Friendships fade.

I found great solace in therapy. My therapist became "my best friend" because I could tell her everything. She didn't judge. She listened for weeks. Weeks turned into months, and soon I was at the one-year mark since I had kissed him goodbye.

I look back and I am amazed by all that I accomplished in the first six months after Larry died.

I handled all the legal matters.

- I met with financial advisors to protect the money I had.
- I put a lot of money into my house to get it on the market and sell it.
- I sent 21 boxes to a shredding event.
- I sent three trailers of junk to the dump.
- I gave most of his power tools to family members.
- I hired a landscape service.
- I hired a consultant to help me pack up everything that belonged to Larry, and she donated it all appropriately.
- I also boxed up everything I did not think I would ever use again and donated those things too.
- I sold my house.
- I wrote four contracts on houses, and the last one was finally accepted.
- I packed more boxes.
- I hired movers.
- I had a huge garage sale.

# FRACTURED

- I moved.
- I unpacked.
- I set up new accounts with utility companies.

Yes, I sold my house and moved into my new home on 9/18/2019, and I took some flak for that decision. However, our home was an unrepaired sinkhole house. It would need a new roof soon. It would need interior painting. The roof on the lanai leaked, and that cost over $3000 to fix. It was four bedrooms and two baths on a large lot, and every time I sneezed I was writing a check for something.

An offer to purchase came in from an investor, and I took it. I moved to a maintenance-free development on a golf course on a small amount of water, and I had peace and nature.

Moving meant dealing with Larry's closet, and I had a friend come to help me. We packed everything up and donated it to a men's shelter.

I still have certain articles of Larry's clothing. I sleep in his T-shirts; I have several of my favorite collared shirts I loved to see him wear; I have his special jewelry, his wedding band, a bottle of his cologne, and many other things. I can sense his energy when I touch these things.

I made a treasure box when I was at a spa in New Mexico, and it sits on his nightstand. There are very special things in it, and I open the box all the time to just gaze and reflect on our life. It sits on top of the parking pass for Brasstown Bald mountain, where we had an exceptional day exploring all the beauty nature provided, and it was our last trip together. Of all the trips we took, this one was the best, the most beautiful, the most fun.

A year after moving into a new home, I moved again. Many people who follow my daily writing know I left Florida. To continue moving forward, I needed to leave.

*"Mature Love is Strengthening.
Mature lovers respect and admire each other, which enables them to be strong, honest, trusting, and unafraid in the presence of each other. There is no shielding from hurt, no holding back, and no manipulation."*
Michael e Cavanagh

Larry let me walk my own journey. While we were joined by marriage and blessed by God, he never tried to change me, to mold me, to make me conform to what his ideas were. He just wanted me to see the best inside me he knew was there.

I learned in time that there was a right way and a wrong way to approach him with a new idea. I am of fiery Hungarian bloodlines; he is of stubborn Polish bloodlines. The two could be oil and water, and explosions did happen. We were both very passionate about our beliefs and about our feelings, and one day we were having a spirited conversation—and because he could talk louder than I could, he used that to prove his point.

He was stepping on my last damn nerve, and I was at my limit; I jumped up in the air and came down pounding my fists on the kitchen counter.

# FRACTURED

He laughed, he couldn't stop laughing, and the spirited conversation was over. I never tried that again, although I probably should have.

Anyone who knew him knew he could yell. I had to stop sharing the same office space with him because when he got irritated curse words could fly, and while curse words never bothered me, it was the decibels they were shouted at that made me cower.

Not only that, but he was a messy person. His desk had papers everywhere, and mine looked like no one worked there. It was one of his quirks, and I just moved out.

One day before we got married we were in the beloved Durango, and Larry was backing out of the garage. Before putting the car in drive, he would adjust his rearview mirror. Did he reach for it and turn it slightly? No; he would tap on the bottom of it in a series of taps that drove me crazy.

I had reached my limit with the tapping. I reached up and twisted the rearview mirror sideways. I waited for his reaction, expecting some snarky remark, but no, he just looked at me and burst into laughter. He had an amazing sense of humor, and he allowed me to poke fun at some of his quirks, but believe me when I say I never used the same tube of toothpaste he used.

I have a favorite poet and she wrote this:

> *At the end of the day, no one will walk your journey for you.*
> *You have to do that.*
> *At the end of the day, no one will dream for you.*
> *You have to do that.*
>
> Nahwa Zedian

I loved his quirks, and when they got to be a little too much, I changed directions. The one quirk he had that I adored was when I changed directions, he always knew where I was, and he was always there behind me.

# 15

# The Anniversaries of the Heart

> "The holiest of holidays are those kept by ourselves in silence and apart: The secret anniversaries of the heart."
> Henry Wadsworth Longfellow

The very first remembrance day for me was Larry's birthday in May. I took a friend out to dinner to a pleasant restaurant neither of us had ever been to before, and we had a lovely evening. I was still living in disbelief, and my brain was numb.

Larry and I celebrated many of his birthdays out of town. We had been on a cruise; we had gone to New Orleans, we even had spent his birthday at Walt Disney World several times. They were all special and very memorable, especially at Walt Disney World, where they give you a pin with your name on it, and all the cast members call you out by name as you pass them and wish you a happy birthday.

The next remembrance day, though, was earth-shattering for me. I planned a road trip in late June to visit girlfriends from north Georgia to Tennessee. It was a lovely trip, and I spent the days talking about Larry, visiting some beautiful places, and the trip began and ended with staying in a cabin in the north Georgia mountains where Larry and I had spent our last vacation together.

I thought I would be just fine driving home on July 1st, only it did not work out that way. July 1st was our wedding anniversary, and as I drove that eight hours of I-75, memory after memory visited me as if they were trailers of upcoming attractions in a movie theater, only nothing would ever be upcoming again.

By the time I got home I was a mess. I don't remember picking Willie up from the kennel. I don't remember if I ate anything that night. The only thing I remember is I had 14 phone calls from friends and family, and those calls got me through.

- In an earlier chapter I suggested that you ask people to call you on these days of remembrance because you don't really want to spend them alone trying to deal with it all.

Years ago I read "Hour of Gold, Hour of Lead" by Anne Morrow Lindbergh and she wrote that "the inexplorably difficult thing in life, particularly in suffering, is to face the truth." The truth is, these days of remembrance will come. The holidays will show up too, and there are things you can do to protect yourself.

I thought I wanted to go home for Thanksgiving, and I did. I felt out of place, and this was absolutely no one's fault. Traditions had changed, I felt like I did not belong there, and sometimes I wonder if maybe they liked Larry better than they liked me. Oh, I know better, but it goes back to the changes that happen when one partner dies and now things are different. I cannot put my finger on what makes everything different, I just knew when I flew back to Florida I needed to have new traditions.

Christmas came knocking right after Thanksgiving, and it was terrible. I decorated my new home. I bought a tree and decorated it. I put out all the great smelling candles Larry and I had bought together. I listened to Christmas music; I watched Hallmark movies, and I thought I was okay.

Gifts arrived from friends and family, and cards came in the mail. I bought a small prime rib roast, and I was sticking with as many traditions as I could. This was a BIG mistake.

I wasn't ready to repeat traditions. In fact, now that I think back on it, I do not want any of those traditions in any future Christmas seasons.

I opened my gifts; I received phone calls; I put my roast in the oven; I watched some movies, and in the early afternoon I took my tree down. I was done; I wanted it gone.

Everything was going well until I couldn't get the sections apart. I became a mad woman. I attacked that tree with all my might and a hammer. I still couldn't take it apart. I threw it into the garage and it laid there on the floor until friends came over to help me dismantle it.

I put the finishing touches on my dinner, and I sat down to eat it at the dining room table—and that is when I fell apart. I couldn't eat. The roast went into the trash, and I sat at the table and cried hard for about an hour.

Since that day, I have done some research about grief and holidays, and these are some ideas I found:

- You might be alone, but remember you are not the only person in this entire world who is alone. I didn't write this to make anyone feel bad, quite the opposite. Sometimes when we stop to realize there are others, we do often feel better.
- It's important to set realistic expectations, and while you think about that know this may be a really good time to

set boundaries. You do not have to do what makes you feel sad. You can say no.
- I wrote about this in an earlier chapter, and here I go again. Reach out to others. I know it may not be something you are comfortable doing, and again you have a choice. You can reach out and perhaps have a wonderful time, or you can stay quiet and allow others to have a wonderful time without you. Remember, others are unsure if they should invite you to something, so putting your thoughts out there, asking questions about plans helps them do the asking.
- Use social media to reach out to others. Do a Zoom call. Connecting may lift your spirits higher than you could have imagined.
- If you are a planner, make a plan.
- I used the word choice, and yes, you have choices to make. You are a grown person; you can decide what you would like to do.
- A big one that I did was I talked to Larry about the Hallmark Christmas movie I would be watching as if he were sitting on the couch next to me. When I put the candles out this year, I lit the ones he liked best. I talked to him about Christmas memories, including the wonderful videos we had on our phones of our dogs.
- You could serve food at a shelter, or give some time to a food pantry, or offer to wrap presents for a charity.
- Whatever you do, please make sure you have some private time if you are out with people, and use this time to do some breathing techniques, deep inhales, slow exhales. These help center you again. Honor your true feelings. If you are not happy where you are, leave. If you are happy

and feeling like it's wrong, stop and breathe again. You deserve happiness.
- Get lost in some music. If you can't bear the seasonal songs, go with music you like. Our brains have a very strong response to music.
- Change your traditions and start new ones. My birthday and Thanksgiving are on the same day this year as I write. I have some planning to do.

I also know that this year, my Christmas will be different. I am not sure if there will be a tree ever again in my house. It's a lot of work for one person and a lot of emotional work too.

*"It's exhausting trying to be stronger than I feel."*
Unknown

The Christmas season of 2018 was filled with excitement. We had a family wedding to attend in South Florida, a weekend filled with laughter and love, and beautiful Christmas decorations.

We spent the weekend soaking up all the excitement, drinking and eating, sitting around a firepit and talking about so many memories, and it was just lovely.

Little did anyone in the family know that this would be the last time we would all be sitting with Larry in our midst hearing his laughter, seeing his eyes sparkle, enjoying the beach, and feeling the December breezes caressing our shoulders.

The following weekend we were the invited guests at a special Christmas concert in downtown Tampa, and as we posed for a group photo, again little did we know that would be our last photo taken together.

I created our traditional Christmas. I filled the house with carols, candles, lights, two trees, cookies, wine, the dogs, and so much love. Every night there was a Hallmark Christmas movie to watch. Larry loved these movies—he was definitely as in love with love as I was.

As I look back, I have caught myself realizing there was a difference in Larry, I knew he was tired. I would ask him about it, and he would change the subject, telling me he was just fine. I can't help but wonder if he was hiding something from me, and wondering about it came easy to me since he had hidden health issues from me in the past.

That was our last Christmas. I don't know that I have the strength to go through another one; it is so difficult when you long for someone you cannot ever have again with you at the most wonderful time of the year.

# 16

# There is No Rule Book

> *"Hell, there are no rules here. We're just trying to accomplish something."*
> Thomas A. Edison

If there was a rule book about grief, I wouldn't be writing my story. There are guides, there are articles online, and there are other books. The bottom line, though, is that we learn by doing in our own time and in our own space.

I want everyone to remember that you are wonderful because you are living each day with pain that other people cannot even fathom. Read that sentence again.

Let's start by acknowledging the fact that we all get up every day and move forward. We may only do one thing that day, and that is okay. We moved forward.

No rules.

I would like to list some suggestions, though. Ready?

- Find something every day to be grateful for, even the smallest thing.
- Move your body every day. Moving your body physically will also move yourself mentally and emotionally.

- Don't let anyone or anything rush you.

That mental or real to-do list is probably overwhelming, so make small goals. Decide on one or two things to do that day. The rest can wait.

- Get outside. Practice some deep and slow breathing while you are out there.
- Get a dose of sunshine as often as you can. Take a walk in it, sit in a garden in it, feel the warmth of the sun falling on the top of your head and your shoulders.
- Have positive people around you.
- Journal. It is so good for you to write your thoughts. I wrote in my journal every day. Even while Larry was in the hospital, I wrote.
- I learned to meditate. Meditation can be deep thinking, you can meditate while walking, or you can listen to guided meditations which can help at night if you are having trouble sleeping.
- Welcome the quiet times.
- Eat for nourishment because you need to eat healthy.
- You are still here for a reason. Please find some gratitude in that.

There will be days, there will be times when all the advice I listed above flies out the window, and that is okay too.

Here are some things I did that might help you and please remind yourself that it is okay to do some of these (or all of these) things.

- Scream in the shower or cry in the car (not while driving).
- It's okay to lose things—we all will. I lost my keys, my phone, my car, my wallet, and my mind, and I am still here and I found everything else.
- I still put things in my refrigerator that should go in my pantry. It's all good.
- Change grocery stores. I had to do that; we'd shopped together, so I changed stores.
- You may look down at your feet and realize you have two different shoes on.
- You can eat cereal for supper.
- It is okay to smell his clothing. I wear his T-shirts to bed.
- You will know the right time to pack things away. Don't rush.
- Say his name out loud and use his name when you talk to your friends. He lived—call him by name.
- It is okay to say NO. Saying no is self-care.
- It is okay to cancel plans.

There are many other things that are okay too. Remember, there are no rules.

I never lost my ability to smile after Larry died. Just seeing a friend who knew us would bring a smile to my face. As time passed, I found it brought me peace to find a reason to smile. I found I could smile and have tears streaming down my face at the same time.

You will in time learn how to be independent. Oh, I know you will fight me on this thought, but you are moving forward, you are making decisions, you are doing it on your own. This makes you independent.

With this independence comes the realization that you have changed. You are stronger now—don't you dare think you are weak because you aren't. You do not need anyone's permission as you move forward, and unless an opinion is coming from an attorney or a financial advisor, ignore the rest. If something, anything, makes your stomach knot up, leave it alone and think about it again later. If your stomach still knots up, tell it to go to hell. Trust your gut.

I heard repeatedly from my friends and followers how I amazed them with my strength, my resilience, and my energy. I wasn't even aware of what I could do until I had very little help and had to handle things on my own. Now I realize I was wearing a cape. I have superpowers. My superpower is I am a widow. You can claim this superpower too.

*"No matter where we come from, there is one language we can all speak and understand from birth, the language of the heart, love."*
Imania Margria

Who among us has not read The Five Love Languages? We were driving to a conference in Orlando, and I read the entire book out loud to Larry.

When we got home again, we sat quietly and determined what our love languages were.

It was no surprise to me that Larry's love languages were words of affirmation and physical touch.

I matched him with words of affirmation, but I knew my second one was acts of service.

Once we made each other aware of our love languages, our relationship deepened (many times because we reminded each other, smiling while we gave reminders).

Larry and I both had baggage when we met, and reading this book together was a brilliant thing to do. People give love the way they wish to receive love.

I made elaborate meals for Larry because I am about acts of service. I told him many times every day how much I loved him, and many times he said it first.

Physical touch was simple, and besides having a wonderful sexual relationship, we held hands everywhere we went. Yes, we had PDA moments. Love is not just for the young.

We worked on our love. It is a wise thing that everyone should do.

# 17

# Your Grief is not My Grief, It's All Yours

> Eeyore: "We can't all, and some of us don't. That's all there is to it."
> Pooh: "Can't all what?"
> Eeyore: "Gaiety. Song-and-dance. Here we go round the mulberry bush."
> A. A. Milne

Everyone grieves differently than anyone else. There is no roadmap, no guidebook, although I have tried to give you one here in this second part of my book.

It is so important to hang on to the people who validate your feelings, and if you are in therapy, this might be your therapist.

There are constant challenges, and each one has the power to kick your feet out from under you and knock you to the floor. Therefore, it is so important to have people who understand in your circle of support.

There were days when I felt I was on that horrible amusement park ride called "Wild Mouse." That terrible version of a roller coaster scared the living daylights out of me as a kid with its turns and twists where I felt the entire car would plunge to the pavement below and I would not make it out alive.

Something would happen, and I would be on that ride again—and then one day I realized I never plunged to the pavement below and that I could slow the ride down by just stepping back and letting go.

It helped me to look for answers. I had worked in many hospitals as a nurse, and I needed more answers than the hand-patting answers some people tried to give me. The day that I sat with a specialist MD in palliative care was the day I had closure. It is the day I understood Larry's brain injury completely.

Reading books on grief, joining grief groups on social media, and honoring your person may help you so much.

There is no timeline. You are not punching a time clock. You are moving forward at your own pace. Allow your mind and your body to guide you. I have been writing this book for a long time, and the push was on to get it done by my writing coach. I took a week off after she pushed me. I just couldn't do it.

I bargained with God so often I was certain heaven had become a flea market of negotiations from the start. "God, if you let this happen, I will do this." I would ask Him how He could divide a perfect union that He had blessed in marriage.

I prayed a lot. I used to kid Larry; I called him my Catholic boy because he told me so many wonderful stories of his childhood, not so wonderful stories about the nuns, and how much he enjoyed being an altar boy. I also kidded him about last rites, and he would always respond that he wanted to die as a Catholic. I honored that wish.

After Larry died, I fell to my knees many times asking God to tell me why this happened. I was certain I was being punished.

Larry died because of something I did to someone or something I did in my past. Then I remembered our God is a forgiving God, and eventually I stopped questioning the why, and I accepted that there was a plan—I just wasn't aware of it yet.

One day I had a sudden inspiration to make what I call a happiness list. I wrote a list of everything that made me happy, and it was time to uncover these things.

This is my list:

- I negotiated an impressive deal on a brand-new car.
- I sold my house to an investor, and I bought a new house all by myself.
- I organized everything that needed to be done to my new house and it all got done in five days before the moving van arrived.
- I had to buy new clothes because I dropped those 25 pounds I had wanted to lose
- I took a trip to New Mexico where I knew no one, and I came back a better woman.
- I started writing this book.
- A year later I realized I wasn't happy living in Florida, and in 2 months I bought/sold/moved/unpacked again in South Carolina.

Whenever I begin to feel down about things, I look at my list, and there are copies of it in various places in my home.

While I know that your life, and my life, and our identities have changed, toward the end of my first year I saw myself differently. I really thought about what is important to me. I meditated and took better care of my body and my health.

# FRACTURED

I got rid of things that were weighing me down physically.

I made a second happiness list, and on this one I wrote the names of people I can count on to talk to, to meet for coffee, to laugh or cry with, and that list is on my desk where I can see those names. My heart fills with gratitude when I see their names.

I recently started a new list for my future. It is difficult for me to stay in one place very long, especially on my own, and I wrote things that will take a lot of thought before making any big decisions.

I could end up in Portugal, who knows? I just know I am not done exploring this world, and I also know that when the time is right, everything will fall into place.

I listen to music all the time. I have it playing as I write; it doesn't bother me. Larry was a country music man; I was light jazz and popular singers of our current times. We both learned to enjoy each other's music styles, and every day I ask my Echo device to play a specific artist. The sad songs, and the songs we loved play often, and I get through them. I cry now and then; other times I just sit back and smile.

I do a lot of deep breathing, especially when something or someone aggravates me. I especially find great relaxing peace when I do Box Breathing. Box Breathing is done by Navy Seals. They have proven it to be useful not only for stress management, but also it can reduce your blood pressure.

It is very simple to do.

1. Let out all the air in your lungs to a count of four.
2. Keep your lungs empty for a count of four.
3. Inhale for a count of four.
4. Keep your lungs full for a count of four.

I visualize the shape of a box as I do this. It will help you with as little as four cycles.

I also look for memories with humor attached to them, and that helps a lot.

*"Will is to grace as the horse is to the rider."*
Saint Augustine

Years ago I entered a contest to win a cruise. I had to write my story and then people voted on it. I worked hard to win, and when I got the phone call telling me I had won, I was excited beyond belief.

Neither of us had ever been on an ocean cruise before, and I was delighted in humming the title song from the movie "Titanic" just to raise Larry's blood pressure a little.

We were on board and sailing off into the sunset, and we were so happy to be there. I had booked shore excursions for us, and our very first one was horseback riding on the beach and into the Caribbean Sea. Larry and I had been riding before, and we were really looking forward to doing this.

They assigned us horses, and the guides were helping us get seated properly on what they call a water saddle. This saddle was about 1 inch thick of canvas-covered foam, and when you sit on a horse wearing a water saddle, the spine of the horse is right in the middle, and you can feel it. It is not too comfortable.

We were all waiting for one last family, and they arrived with Granny. This woman had to be about 80 years old, and the guides kept asking her family if they were sure she would be okay. I was getting concerned, and I was right to be concerned because they put this family right ahead of me and Granny fell off her horse.

Larry was ahead of me and did not see all this happening, but my horse did. It got spooked and took off galloping through the water. There I was on a one-inch foam saddle bouncing up and down. It was painful and frightening.

The guides were yelling for me to pull back on my reins and stop this speeding horse. I was. I had ridden enough times to know how to stop a horse, but this horse wasn't stopping.

I had no clue where Larry was now; I only knew if this horse did not stop we would be on the other side of the island. Then the horse stopped. I looked back at the people who were all congregated where we had first started, which was about a quarter mile down the beach. I dismounted and left the horse in the water.

The guides were now yelling at me to get the horse. I yelled back, "Get your own f---ing horse." That was the end of our shore excursion that day.

Larry and I often looked at pictures of us on horseback and laughed. It wasn't very funny when it happened but it created a great memory.

# 18

## Slaying the Grief Dragon

*"It is impossible for you to go on as you were before, so you must go on as you never have."*
Cheryl Strayed

I often look at one of the many framed photos I have of Larry in my home, and I tell him this:

"Sweetheart, on 2/19/19 you laid down your sword. On 3/3/19 I picked it up in preparation of slaying the grief dragon."

I will never put grief in the ground, but I learned how I can have delightful days that outnumber the awful days. One day it just all changed, ever so slightly, but the change was welcome.

As I journeyed through my wilderness, I saw flashes of sunlight appearing. I knew that these glimmers were coming to me because I was reaching a new level in my grief. The pathway in my wilderness had started a gentle uphill climb. Sunlight was peeking through the cragginess of the large rocks.

I was working with a new therapist because I had been diagnosed with PTSD. Those of us who witness a sudden death often have trauma. One day in a session my therapist told me I should think of grief as being a "thing" attached to me at the hip.

# FRACTURED

It puzzled me at first, but then he said, "Your grief thing goes with you everywhere, so maybe it is time to introduce it to your sunny side of life instead of allowing this thing to keep you in the darkness all the time."

My therapist asked me to picture my grief attached to me and talk to it as if it was an actual person. As odd as this all sounds, once I started doing this, I had better days. Grief has shown me I was still inside my physical body. It has also let me know that I can yell at it, and it doesn't get even. Sometimes I even visualize it as an opponent, and I am kickboxing with it and winning.

You will know when or if you are ready to take your grief with you, to identify it and even yell at it because it is an authentic part of you and your life. My grief has taught me some wonderful things.

One day you might realize that the painful memories don't hurt as much as they once did. You feel okay with being alone, and you no longer rely on the need for distractions. You are not as sensitive as you once were, and words don't pierce your heart as they used to do.

I found I could talk to other people who were grieving, and it felt good to help them. Or maybe you go to church and you get through the entire service without a tear.

You no longer feel exhausted, and you are eating and sleeping better. You find things to be grateful for, and maybe you have even started a gratitude journal.

I was making new friends, and I enjoyed their company. My confidence came back, and I was okay with my new identity.

I found I was crying less and laughing more (mostly at funny television shows), and I made plans to do things and go places.

Back in Chapter 7, I wrote this: *Grief is not your friend—or is it?* I said I would explain that thought later in this book. Well, this is what I found. While grief is not my bosom buddy, I have learned to take it with me everywhere, and when it wants to make its presence known I am strong enough now to tell it to zip its lips. I may still have to do some Box Breathing, but I can wrestle grief to the ground.

Again, there is no timeline regarding when you will feel better. I am older, and perhaps a little wiser, and I know the woman who Larry fell in love with, and she was a joyful woman. That has helped me immensely in my healing journey.

Will I ever stop grieving? Hell to the no. This man was the love of my life. He was a gift given to me, and I will tell you about that in Part 3 of this book. I cry a little almost every day. I miss him so much, and I accept the fact that the forever we promised each other has different end dates. He died loving me fiercely. You can bet your last dollar I honor that love, and I am grateful that I had a man who loved me so deeply every day of my life.

In bringing Part 2 of this book to a close and moving on to *The Legacy of Love and Life with Carole and Larry*, which is just a title I made up as I wrote, I wanted to make sure I had shared everything I set out to share. As I looked back, I saw that while I had hit my major points, there is always more to write, but I had to stop somewhere, and I was happy with what I had written this far.

"Sometimes an angel, sometimes a hell raiser, always a strong woman."
R H Sin

# FRACTURED

Once upon a time my mother told me I was the strongest woman she knew. It was one of the kindest things she ever said to me, because she wasn't a loving mother.

All of us have been through a lot in our lives. Every one of us could have a Lifetime Channel movie made about everything we have been through.

In the 20+ years I spent with Larry, I didn't have to rely on my strength. He was my rock. He took the blows handed to me. He made them better.

When I had to have breast biopsies three different times, he was always there.

He rarely scared me. He was a beast. I had called him that over the years because he always got back up. He always showed how determined he was to be my caretaker. If he holds any disappointment at this moment, it would be that he left me alone to handle so much shit. He would feel terrible about it.

The first time he scared me was when he had unstable angina and needed a stent. The second time he scared me was when he came in from doing yard work and told me he should probably call a doctor on Monday.

I looked at him and asked him why he needed one, and he said he was having chest pain. He scared me. I drove him to the ER.

Four days later he was discharged from the hospital with another stent placement.

We got past being scared until his cardiologist explained that he still had a blockage and that this blockage was beyond the area he had placed a stent.

That is when we faced a double bypass surgery, and again I was scared.

Later on the day of that surgery, he started to bleed internally. Now I was really scared.

Why is it that the three times this man scared me so badly it had to do with his loving heart?

The night he had the stroke led to 13 days of terror followed by months of being scared.

I learned in a therapy session to call up the happiest day of my life whenever I felt deeply sad.

When the therapist asked me what that day was, my answer was the day Larry and I got married.

I do not have to get our wedding album out to recall any part of that day. I can see it clearly in my memories as if it happened yesterday.

# Part 3

# 19

## 30 Years of Waiting

> Alice: "How long is forever?"
> White Rabbit: "Sometimes just one second."

My parents used to tell me I was in love with love. I was. I wouldn't agree with them then, but I can look back and see I really was in love with love.

There was a special woman in my life who was also in love with love, and she would take me downtown, and we would crash weddings in Old Stone Church right off Public Square in downtown Cleveland. I find a lot of joy in those memories because we crashed more than one wedding starting when I was six or seven years old, and I was 13 when we crashed the last one.

She was my loving grandmother, my father's mother, and she had the sweetest smile. Her eyes would squint up when she smiled, and she would put a finger to her lips as she opened the doors to the church, and we would sit in the last pew.

Hell yes, I was in love with love. My grandmother exposed me to it at an early age, and crashing weddings became an annual happening. I would go to spend a week with her in the summer, and on Saturday morning we would take the bus and be uninvited guests at someone's wedding.

I fooled my mother by telling her I needed to take a dress and my patent leather shoes every visit, allowing her to believe we went to church. We did—we just didn't go on Sundays.

I felt as if I were living in a fairy tale. Brides wore voluminous gowns back then, and I would sit in a pew dreaming of falling in love and being a beautiful bride.

I never had the chance to ask my grandmother why she enjoyed it so much, and one day I just thought she probably was in love with love as well.

*A Summer's Day in June 1999*
*"I ask you to pass through life at my side—to be my second self, and best earthly companion."*
Charlotte, Bronte, *Jane Eyre*

We had fallen in love hard and fast. We met in December 1998 and moved in together two months later. There was no turning back. I knew Larry checked off all the boxes, and my number one need was to have someone whom I could trust to always be there for me as others had not.

Larry and I both had a history and a lot of baggage from failed marriages and relationships.

Years later we would laugh about the fact that I had proposed to him first, probably in April when we met for drinks at a local restaurant and I asked him point-blank if we were on the same page, that page being a serious relationship leading to marriage.

That took a lot of courage on my part because this relationship was so new, and it could have gone the other way if my boldness scared him off. It didn't. He told me we were definitely on the same page.

One afternoon in June, we were sitting outside on the patio and talking about the upcoming weekend when he just asked if I would like to marry him. I didn't really hear his words because he made his proposal part of a general conversation.

Larry looked at me and said, "Carole, will you marry me?" I was so surprised because I didn't see this coming. He looked at me and said, "I will not ask you a third time."

That was his proposal. He didn't get down on one knee; he did not have a ring for me yet; it did not matter because our love filled our world with sunshine and flowers. This man asked me to be his wife, and elation filled my heart and finally being in love with love had worked for me. He was sitting there smiling from ear to ear, and we both had tears rolling down our cheeks.

Only six months earlier, I had been talking about wanting to meet a man that would care for me like no other had. I spread that word everywhere, and one day a friend invited me to attend a church service where a Burning Bowl Ceremony was an annual event. I wrote what I wanted on a piece of paper, the entire congregation said many prayers, and we all asked God to help us find what we were seeking.

Less than a month later, I met Larry. I have always known he was a gift from God, because God knew that I needed Larry in my world. He had heard my prayers, and He had read my note asking for the love of a man who would always take care of me.

# 20

## Day 77

> *"The trouble is you think you have time."*
> Gautama Buddha

I have mentioned several times in this book I write my feelings every day and post them on Facebook. Day 77 was May 7th, and what I wrote showed up as a memory. I read it and knew it fit right into my story. A friend said that what I wrote is a perfect description of my feelings that day.

Day 77 and it's Tuesday. I woke this morning at 3:40AM wondering if Larry knew that when he took me to the mountains to give me the gift of that experience that it would live forever in my heart.

In retrospect, those of us closest to him saw the physical changes since his open heart surgery.

He had visibly aged over the past year.

His cardiologist kept telling him he needed to slow down based on his test results.

Larry came out of that surgery with a fresh problem: cardiomyopathy. His heart pumped blood with more efficiency before the surgery than after. In fact, there is a percentage that the doctors go by, and pre-surgery Larry's percentage was 65 percent;

post-op it was 35 percent. In medical terms it is called an ejection fraction and the results let doctors know how much blood is ejected from the left ventricle with each heartbeat.

No one ever explained why that happened to him. Larry always dug deep for answers, and when the question was medical, I joined in.

Larry rarely complained, and if he was feeling off he wouldn't tell me, or maybe it just came on so slowly that he did not notice it.

He kept doing everything he always did. He pushed the envelope, though. When I asked him to hire a landscape company, he would say, "No, they don't clean up the clippings." When I asked him to hire a tree-trimming service, he would tell me, "They don't know the right time to clip the palm fronds."

The weekend before he had his stroke he trimmed all the crepe myrtle trees even though I'd asked him to let them go. In fact, we argued about that.

The night he had the stroke, he went out to feed the rose bushes, and we had not finished dinner yet.

I had the roses pulled and taken away after he died. I couldn't look at them.

His son used the word "driven" to describe him.

His daughter told me when we dated that once he got started on a project nothing would stop him, and she was correct.

He was a proud man, first of his family to go to college, and it is no surprise he was an engineer.

Do I think he knew that he was starting to slow down? I think he suspected that the surgery had left him with the short straw in life but he kept going.

Larry never once planned a trip for us. We used to get an idea and plan together. It was a Sunday in August when he brought his laptop out to the kitchen and said, "I want to take you to the north Georgia mountains this fall where you can feel as if we are in a Hallmark movie" (in love in a small town). As sappy as some think those movies are, Larry liked them a lot because Larry loved loving me and making my eyes sparkle.

It was a perfect trip. He did good. We had Paris twice; we had Hawaii; we had many islands in the Caribbean; we had other fabulous trips, but the best trip of all was that October.

He knew enough to do this for me.

And he would drive into town every morning to bring me coffee from Cabin Coffee Co. It was almost as good as the coffee he made me at home.

*"We'll always have Paris."*
the movie *Casablanca*

Larry began to write his award-winning book "Which Food Which Wine" before we married, and we even talked about it on our honeymoon. The book was important to him. He would tell me it was his legacy.

He wrote, I edited, and it went to the publisher. I will never forget the day a semi-truck pulled up to unload 1000 copies. We both poured so much work and time into that book. Now it was here, and that meant marketing and attending book fairs to boost interest in it.

What I didn't know is that while we were doing all this marketing, Larry had submitted a copy to Gourmand International World

Cookbooks to be considered for their 2002 awards until one day a letter came letting us know that his book was in the contest and the awards would be held in Angers, France in February 2003.

We looked at each other, booked a flight, a car, and a hotel, and we left for France.

In the 20+ years I spent with Larry, this was his proudest moment—other than the day we were married, of course. He was like a child in a candy store. He was so excited, and it was all he could talk about.

We flew into Charles De Gaulle, managed (without speaking French) to pick up our rental car, and drove to Angers. We were thrilled to be in France, the countryside was so beautiful, and the toll road was $21 one way—sticker shock.

We found the hotel, and Larry let me out of the car to ask about parking. I let him know where to park, and he drove off to find the alley that would take him behind the hotel. It never had occurred to me that this man who had worked as a high-rise engineer on the Sears Tower would get lost. He did. He got lost for 45 minutes, and my heart was upside down in my chest beating wildly.

Larry finally stopped and asked someone for the Blue Marina Hotel. He was close to having the name correct, it was the Hotel Blue Marine. A kind Frenchman pointed him to the correct avenue, he finally pulled up, and we allowed the bellman to park the car.

We spent the next several days exploring the charming town of Angers. We shopped and shopped, and I was coming home with a suitcase of beautiful clothes, including a rain jacket I still wear.

We found lovely restaurants, and we drank a lot of wine.

The contest is held by Edouard Cointreau, since the Cointreau factory is located in Angers. We had a lovely tour, we bought some Cointreau, and we sampled other liquors bottled there.

We made beautiful memories, and we met so many wonderful people on this trip. The most charming of all was Edouard Cointreau. We had dinner underground in caverns in February and we were treated to a delicious meal.

This interesting restaurant is located in the town of Rochemenier. What an interesting dinner in the underground of rock formations. I cannot remember if there was indoor plumbing or if we had to leave the caverns, but since they cook and some live in these caverns, I would assume it was indoors.

The name of this restaurant is Restaurant Les Caves de la Genevraie SN.

And the bread...oh, that bread.

What a trip it was, two Americans navigating French roads and towns.

Larry didn't speak a word of French, and I could get by with my ability to speak in the first person. With the wine flowing, we understood each other.

The magical night arrived, and they drove us to the breathtaking Chateau de Brissac.

I found this description of the amazing night on the Gourmand International website:

> *2003 Loire Valley, Angers*
>
> *Chateau de Brissac, Loire Valley. The Marquis de Brissac hosted the event, with many star chefs and friends, including Edouard Carlier of Beauvilliers in Paris. Chef Wan was back, following a new trend of past event stars coming back to a yearly event of friendship, fun and business.*

*The book of the year was "Essential Cuisine" by Michel Bras. The wine star was Rene Renou, President of INAO and member of the Gourmand French jury. This was a very elegant and glamorous event that set the awards apart from all other events of the sector. The Australian Ambassador to France was there, with Maurice de Rohan, Agent General for South Australia, the perfect gentleman and friend, who did not miss any Gourmand events.*

*Chateau de Brissac is 7 floors tall with over 200 rooms, and the 13th duke de Brissac and his family live there. It is the tallest castle in France.*

On the night of the awards they treated us to a seven-course dinner with a different wine with each dish.

We also met the duke, and many of us were unsure what we were supposed to do. I dropped a small curtsey; he kissed my hand.

The awards ceremony began, hosted by Chef Wan of Malaysia, who is a television celebrity chef there and a total delight. He was so entertaining.

Larry and I both knew the event was drawing to a close. Edouard Cointreau stepped up to the microphone and all I remember (after seven glasses of wine) was Larry's name being called out. Larry went up to make his thank-you speech, and I grabbed our camera to take pictures. I tripped and the camera went flying, scattering the batteries; however, I did get one photo, which we cherished.

"Life with Carole is always fun," as Larry would say from time to time.

We left Angers for Paris, with a side trip to Chartres as I had studied the cathedral there, knowing Rodin would sit on a curb and gaze at the magnificence of this cathedral. That made it difficult to leave because I could feel his presence.

Later when we visited the Rodin Museum to view his work "The Gates of Hell" and "The Thinker," I could sense Rodin's admiration for Chartres Cathedral.

We spent the next week in Paris and Normandy. We used the Metro, we toured museums, we took a fabulous train ride to Normandy, and we wept openly at the cemetery. We stood in the bunkers feeling the war, hearing the gunfire, and seeing the bodies fall.

We felt the energy of Versailles and marveled at the opera house and the Hall of Mirrors.

We were both in awe of being there, and we promised we would return.

Two years later we did just that for Christmas and New Year's Eve. We had Paris—twice.

# 21

## Love Cannot Be Downsized

> *"Love knows not its own depth until the hour of separation."*
> Kahlil Gibran

I know life and love has blessed me. I know that there are people who wish they had the love Larry and I shared. I know because they told me. I know that Larry's love was the greatest gift I ever received. These things push me to never stop talking about him.

So I talk about him…

I talk about him because nothing says I cannot talk about him.

I talk about him because I know him better than anyone else does.

I talk about him even though it hurts; it is part of my healing.

I talk about him because we belong to each other, and nothing will ever change that.

I talk about him because I love him. Every emotion I feel, every emotion inside of me still lives because he loved me.

I talk about him because he lived and deserves to be remembered, and he is only ever a breath away from me.

I know that in grief no one is coming to save me. No one will process all that I go through. I have to do it all on my own, and so

# FRACTURED

do you. You can find a way; I promise you can. Search for it, and activate it when you find it. It is all on you.

I know there is pain and only you can decide how much pain, how long the pain lasts, or when it is time to admit that you are vulnerable. It is so hard to have to tell someone that you just can't get out of bed today because that is not the normal you. Who gives two shits? Maybe this is the normal you today.

We cannot go through life telling lies about how we really feel. We say we are "okay" or "fine," and we are not. Refusing to feel your grief will only inhibit your ability to move forward or sometimes on some days prevent you from pushing forward.

I told people from the very beginning that I would write this book. It took me a while to give myself permission to begin, but when I did, the words and ideas just poured out of my head.

I have done some healing in small ways. I have used my pain to help others. I think things through much better now, and I handle the curve balls thrown at me without wanting to hit something or someone.

Larry met, fell in love, and married a happy woman. I honor him every day by working at being happy.

*Love letters straight from your heart.*
Etta James

August 9, 2000

My dearest Carole,

You stumbled into my life late for our first date. We had a very short date but little did we know that date was going to last a lifetime. Since you have come into my life I have never smiled, laughed or felt so good about myself or most importantly never LOVED someone as I love you. There are times when you are sleeping and I look at you with a thrill in my heart that I have never felt before. I enjoy it so much when you come into the kitchen in the morning and we have breakfast together. Coming home at the end of the day is such a joy because I know you will be there looking for that hug and kiss from me. I enjoy holding you so much that I can't find the words to describe the joy I get when I hold you. All the things in my life are so much more meaningful now that I have you. You are the answer to my prayers. (You are) the kind of woman I prayed for, a kind, considerate, worthy wife, friend, lover and companion one who I can share life's secrets with. One who I can share my goals with. The one I enjoy listening to her goals and desires. I know you'll be there for me as I am there for you. Your love I will cherish forever until forever is as far as I will go. You, my dear one, my true love, my soulmate, my forever partner, my forever lover, my forever into eternity.

I love you sweetheart with my whole being.

Love,

Larry

# 22

## The Wisdom I Have Found in This

> *"Everyone can master a grief but he that has it."*
> William Shakespeare

It is absolutely flipping easy for people to spout out advice when you are carrying grief in your heart. Some will think they know exactly what you should do, others just "tsk tsk" behind your back, and then there are those who walk on eggshells around you.

If only we had the courage when this happens to speak up, but most of us don't. Oh, we always think of what we should have said, and we kick ourselves afterwards for not saying those things.

I wander in my wilderness of grief every day. The knowledge that I have gained a modicum of wisdom came when I saw sunlight instead of gray skies in this wilderness. When sunlight appeared I knew I was gaining wisdom with it too.

When Larry had his stroke, I was numb. I was a zombie. I was out of touch, and out of tune. I lost my vision; I lost my hearing; I lost my voice. I was lost in a black hole.

The day the funeral director called to let me know that Larry was ready to come home was when I started to climb out of that black hole. It is when I felt the horrible pain. It was when I got extremely pissed off. It was when I cried uncontrollably, gasping for air. It was when I asked God to take me too. I didn't want to breathe without Larry.

I can't even remember what I looked like then. Was I putting makeup on, was I fixing my hair, did my shirt match my shorts?

I know I kept myself very busy, so busy because I hated that black hole and did not want to go back there again. Friends and family came to help me, and I am sure they wondered where the sad, grieving Carole was. She was there; she was just back to being a zombie again.

My rock was gone. He had splintered and disintegrated, and he was now reduced to ashes. I couldn't touch him, see him, hold him, love him, or hear his voice.

It wasn't until weeks went by that I realized I did not have to be busy all the time, and I did not have to be strong every damn day. It was perfectly okay to fall apart, to kick a bed pillow, to cry in the shower, to fall to my bed asking him to come back to me.

I didn't know who I was, so how could I possibly be wise? I lost a lot of my identity. We were a married couple; we rarely went anywhere without the other. I took Willie in for her shots in May, and the vet tech looked at me with that *Where's Larry, where's Corky?* look. I burst into tears. I told her they were together, but not here any longer.

And I wrote. I wrote every day. I put everything I wrote on Facebook. Every morning I shared my feelings, my pain, my thoughts, my life, and my fears. As I wrote, I realized writing was my new purpose. It is what I was born to do. After all, didn't I excel at writing in elementary school?

Thankfully, nothing bad happened. I made a lot of decisions and sometimes I changed my mind too. I spent too much money to repair a roof, and I had a handyman take advantage of me, but all-in-all I came through it all pretty much unscathed.

I took an eight-day road trip, and every night I was in a bed in the house of a friend. I was brave enough to hit the road; I just didn't want to spend lonely nights in a motel. I flew back to my hometown to let a dear friend take care of me for a long weekend, and it was just what I needed.

In the fall I boarded a flight to Santa Fe, New Mexico to spend a week at an experiential spa, and that was the best thing I did for myself in those first months. While I was at this spa, I had a session with a licensed family therapist, and he told me I had PTSD. No one had ever said that to me before, and I was relieved because now I knew I could receive treatment for it.

I spent hours with healers and licensed therapists there, and when I cried, they cried. One session had me sitting in a large chair surrounded by soft fluffy pillows. I was covered with a blanket as I told my story. That was my first experience with a therapy known as somatic experiencing.

Somatic experiencing is an alternative therapy being used to treat PTSD. That session where I was bundled up like a baby worked. As I told my story, I was guided in other directions, and when it was all done, I could sense the change in me. I knew I was less traumatized. She gave me tools to use anytime I felt myself slipping back into the trauma zone, and these tools worked.

I knew I had needed to reach out. My heart had been telling me this. I needed to be with old friends and make new ones. I also knew if I sat back and waited for invitations from people, I might grow old waiting. I initiated going out. I wrote about that in an earlier chapter. If you are lonely, you need to be the person who does the inviting if you want to be included. Take a deep breath and make that phone call.

Along the way, I also learned quickly that I had to learn how to do things myself or throw money at whatever it was. YouTube has wonderful videos that can show you how to do most things. I do not climb ladders; I pay a handyman to change my air filters, lightbulbs, smoke detectors, and more.

When I came back from New Mexico, I told my therapist I had been diagnosed with PTSD. My therapist told me that a research grant had been awarded to a local college to study grief and treat it with a newer therapy known as Accelerated Resolution Therapy, abbreviated as ART.

I was interviewed, and I fit their criteria for being in this study. My entire pattern of grief changed when I went into treatment.

ART has been used successfully for over eight years with veterans who have been diagnosed with PTSD. ART was created to help people who have experienced trauma. The protocol that is delivered is meant to bring up original traumatic experiences and change the way the information is ultimately stored. This is the definition I got from www.acceleratedresolutiontherapy.com

I highly encourage anyone who is reading this book to do your own research on this as it is being used in other diagnoses with success too.

I wanted to get better. I wanted to be happier more often. Remember, I stated that Larry met and married a joyful woman.

One session was behind me, and I came home and tried to trigger my trauma and I couldn't. For almost a year, if I were to talk about the night Larry had his stroke, I would fall apart and have difficulty breathing. One session in and I could talk about the entire night without tears.

It works rapidly. Many people are successfully treated in 4-6 sessions.

Over the next four appointments, I relived and received treatment for other traumas in my life. Again, I wasn't able to trigger the trauma to return.

I felt guilty at first because I thought I had been chosen to cry every day for the rest of my life because I am a widow. I cry. I just don't have those belly heaving spasms I used to have. I can talk about Larry's last 13 days without pain. I still mourn, I still grieve, but I am better now, and Larry would want this for me.

I look back now at all the progress I have made, and I know I am much wiser. I know I am an improved version of the old me. I can still have terrible days; I just have new tools in my grief toolbox now to help me get through and feel better.

*"Knowing yourself is the beginning of all wisdom."*
Aristotle

It was on our second date that I told Larry that I was a five-year survivor of breast cancer. This is a tough thing to tell a guy when you are just starting to date. I just felt if it would put a damper on things, sooner was better than later.

It didn't affect him at all. In fact, this wise man did his research, and he asked me a lot of questions about my health. He wanted to know if I was eating properly, if I was exercising, if I was getting my check-ups, and I was pleased to answer all his questions.

Larry truly knew himself much better than I did then, and he was willing to go the distance with me starting with his first 5K in October 1999. We walked it with a friend of mine who was also a breast cancer survivor, and he raced ahead as we approached the finish line to yell and cheer as we approached walking to Tina Turner's song "Simply the Best." I remember crying because who would have ever thought a sea of ladies in pink T-shirts would receive all that applause for ever having had breast cancer.

Larry was wise enough to go to every doctor's appointment with me. He went to every mammogram. When I needed an MRI, he went. I had three more biopsies over the years. He was there.

I had been speaking about breast cancer for many years, and I was giving a talk on it at an organization one day. At the end of my talk, I was asked if I wanted to join a team and walk with this team in the Breast Cancer 3 Day, which is 60 miles of walking over 3 days.

I felt like the world stopped spinning because I am not a woman who wants to sweat, and we lived in Florida now. I also did not like to ask people for money because walkers had to raise a certain amount of money to enter this event.

I took a deep breath and said I would do it. Larry just looked at me because he knew what I was thinking, but again wisdom prevailed, and he didn't ask me why I'd agreed to do this.

I signed up, and I started letting people know that I needed donations, and I decided to make it down and dirty quickly. I told everyone I wanted $100 donations only. I got close to 70 of those donations in less than a week.

Now came the training. No one can just get up and walk 60 miles over three days in 90 degree heat and high humidity without training.

# FRACTURED

During this training I had to have a minor surgical procedure done on my foot. Larry was there. After my foot healed, he presented me with all the research he had done on proper footwear, ideas to prevent blisters, and now he was my wise coach.

We bought the shoes. He applied tincture of Benzoin on my feet all three mornings, and then he patiently wrapped my feet with duct tape, being careful not to overlap the tape, and careful not to leave any gaps. Yes, he was a wise man.

Then he dusted my feet with Gold Bond powder, helped me with my socks, and then he helped me with my shoes. There is a proper way to put your running shoes on for a distance run or walk.

He would cheer me on along the way, and he was at every rest stop, where he would help me change my shoes to a fresh pair all three days.

When I crossed the finish line on Day 3, he was standing there with a dozen pink roses and there I was sweating so much my clothes were stuck to me, I had a tear-stained face, and I thought to myself that Larry was a very wise man for falling in love with me. You see, I fell in love and married a man who was also very happy.

# 23

## Rock Steady

> *"And we begin to rock steady*
> *Steady rocking all night long*
> *And we begin to rock steady*
> *Rocking till the break of dawn"*

Rock Steady" is a single released by American group The Whispers, from their eighteenth studio album *Just Gets Better with Time* (1987). It was produced by the production duo Antonio "L.A." Reid & Kenneth "Babyface" Edmonds. (from Wikipedia)

Music was a big part of our romance, our love, our wedding, our life, and yes, our intimate times.

I think most people walking this earth have intimate moments or memories that include music.

"Rock Steady" wasn't really a song that rang our chimes, so to speak. It was a song that got us up off our chairs wherever we were, and we would dance to it. It has the perfect beat, and okay, it has a sexual feeling to it, I get that, but it was our dance song.

Larry could dance. He owned a high intensity dance club for years outside Chicago, and he liked dance music a lot. One of his favorites was "You Dropped a Bomb on Me" by the Gap Band. We danced to that song often. And there were more dance moments because I liked "Brick House." Oh yes, we had a collection of long play dance songs, and if they led to the floor or the bedroom, that is how we rocked steady.

Larry's favorite singers were Country/Western, and I enjoyed most of them too. There are many beautiful CW love songs, and we used several in our wedding dance selection with "Forever's As Far As I'll Go" by Alabama and "Love of My Life" by Sammy Kershaw was our wedding dance song.

I got to choose our processional; it was "Unexpected Song" by Andrew Lloyd Webber from his Broadway show "Song and Dance" and I chose both Sarah Brightman and Michael Crawford's versions. I felt it was a song that held deep meaning for our love story that had started unexpectedly.

Larry never minded if I took music in a new direction in our lives. He developed a fondness for singers of love songs and songs sung in different languages. That is when Andrea Bocelli and Josh Groban became part of our music choices. If they had concerts on PBS, we watched. If they were in town, we went.

Now I listen to their songs all the time. I thought it would be difficult, but their songs comforted me. Tears fall down my cheeks, but our love was so deep that I can pull the beautiful memories out of every song. I glide back in time to the days when he held me with my head against his chest and his arms around my waist, and we would dance. We danced many Saturday nights away on our lanai or in the kitchen, and in the rest of the house.

I admit there are some songs that make the tears flow freely, especially when Garth sings "The Dance" or "If Tomorrow Never Comes" because that song got Larry talking about my going on without him. It was one of the few times he would allow himself to consider whether one of us would leave ahead of the other. He would always ask me if I could truly feel his love, and if I would really knew how much I was loved. He would cry. The answer is that I absolutely knew how much he loved me.

I can't help but feel that he is crying as I write this because he gets it. I knew he would lay down his life, put his jacket in a puddle or carry me over that same puddle if he didn't have a jacket on. He was that kind of man with that much love.

Imagine how surprised I was when I got in the car one day to drive to the Social Security office with proof that Larry had died, and as I started my car "Rock Steady" started to play. All I could do was sit there and see him dancing with me. I could see every sexy move he ever made. Music and dance was what made our story so sensual. We would see people watching us on the dance floor—they knew, they felt it. We had passion for all those years, and we both deserved it because we had never had it that good before, and there were no rude interruptions by kids, just the dogs.

"And suddenly all the love songs were about you."
Unknown

#  FRACTURED

It only took a month to fall deeply in love, and every morning there would be beautiful emails in my inbox. An engineer is not necessarily a person who can express love in words; however, finding beautiful things to send me was something this engineer excelled in, and every email was special.

Larry found a site that he could personalize, attach a song, and each one sent my heart soaring.

"Come with me and walk on the beach of life and share all our experiences together" was matched with The Platters singing "Only You."

Several days later he wrote, "You are the only one that can bring out a song in my heart and make me feel like I never felt before. I love you so very much, Carole," and his song choice was "Unchained Melody" by the Righteous Brothers.

These love emails went back and forth, and I had no clue he had printed them off and saved them until he wasn't here with me any longer.

Maybe we stopped, I don't know, but I treasure the ones I have from the engineer who had a very romantic side.

Then there were all the cards that he gave me for different occasions. These cards were filled with his loving thoughts.

However, none of the romantic gestures Larry ever made can top the one he gave me on February 23, 2019 when I got into his hospital bed with him and he put his arm around me and rubbed my back and my neck and then to the song we chose for our wedding dance he brought his hand up to my head and caressed my curls. This was his most beautiful gesture, the one that said he loved me with all his heart but that he had to leave.

# 24

# #Superlove

> "And then my soul saw you and it kind of went, 'Oh, there you are. I've been looking all over for you.'"
> Unknown

I had been on a continuous search for that which I never found: the elusive love of my life. When I was dealing with my breast cancer diagnosis, I had the good fortune to be in traumatic diagnosis therapy with a wonderful social worker. She told me I needed to stop giving the great guys away.

This puzzled me, and she took my hands, looked me straight in the eyes, and said, "The next time you meet a marvellous man and you think which single girlfriend you could introduce him to, stop that thinking immediately. You see, if he is good enough for your friend, he is definitely good enough for you."

I filed that advice away and promptly was in a relationship with a man I should have given away.

Fast forward five years, and I heard myself thinking I should introduce Larry to… And I stopped right there.

I had been looking for Larry all my adult life. It took me 30 years to find him and the love he had to give, and I was going to introduce him to someone else? No. I came to my senses.

When we met, I was intrigued. I liked him. I could tell he was one of the good guys, white hat, white bandana, and a white horse. However, a spark was missing.

The truth is that I wasn't allowing the spark to light the fire that would result in smoldering embers of true love because along the way I had been damaged enough to believe I did not deserve what was standing right in front of me.

I was broken. I felt unworthy.

Then one day it hit me that Larry was everything I had been looking for in a life partner. I had asked God to send me the gift of a man I could rely on, a man I could trust with my heart, a man who would always take care of me, and there he was.

I had been having problems making the leap from hoping I would find someone to believing I had found someone. I had a duel going on inside my heart and my head between the words hope and faith.

I had been hoping all those years, and hoping led me right to Larry. I almost did not see that hope and become faith until I heard my therapist's words from five years ago. That was the kick in the ass I needed.

Hope when you reduce it down to its simplest definition is a feeling of expectation. We all say that we hope something will happen. Faith, though, is different; it is belief and trust that it will happen. There is a difference. Once I learned it, I could see how it physically manifested itself in my life. Hope would make me think *Oh please, oh please, oh please,* and I could see myself popping a sweat. Faith is a way of believing that something can happen in the future.

Faith whispered in my ear, *It is here now*. Faith gives you relief because you realize everything happened just the way you had hoped. Faith cannot exist without hope.

I had hoped for years that a man of Larry's caliber would fall into my life, and through the miracle of technology and online dating services, it all came together.

Thirty years. It took 30 years, and we only had 20 years to explore every nuance of what made us both so special to each other.

Thirty years of mistakes.

Thirty years of unhappiness.

Thirty years of loneliness.

Thirty years of tears.

I was done, despite those who wanted to make me all undone for one night, or one week, and leave me in a crumpled mess on the floor.

My energy was gone, spent by those who did not want to stay, and just when I felt used up, the man I called a beast found me. He was captivated, mystified, and intrigued, as if I were the finest wine he had ever brought to his lips and had until now, never tasted.

He got down on the floor with me. All the love he had longed for encircled him like a ring of fire, and eventually that ring of fire surrounded me, and we could see forever in each other's eyes.

Loving each other was better than anything or anyone who had come before. His forever ended, leaving me to lie on the floor where the rings of fire had once burned extinguished by my tears.

My beloved husband, Lawrence F. Sanek.

5/14/46—3/3/19 he lived his dash very well.

# Epilogue
## And so it goes on...

*Being deeply loved by someone gives you strength, while
loving someone deeply gives you courage.*
Lao Tsu

I went through so much, I accomplished so much, and as my days became freer from all that I had been painstakingly doing, my brain opened to allow deep thoughts to speak to me.

I was sitting outside with a glass of wine reflecting on our love for each other when I experienced a deeply profound thought. This thought perched on the bistro tabletop where I was sitting and waited for me to allow it to percolate and become a huge aha moment.

It was then that I realized that I was only meant to have Larry for the 20 years I had him. He was a gift to me, and no matter how many times I wept over the fact that the forever he had promised me was not the forever he gave me, until that moment I didn't understand that he had reached his forever. His work was done.

During our 20 years, he taught me courage and how to bravely stand up to those who would tear me down. He taught me what I am worth and how to embrace my worth every day of my life. He taught me that no matter who or what had come before that I was capable of handling my life without him in it. I knew then that he had left me with years of his love ahead of me still. I was his last great love, and I take so much solace in that fact.

I feel his love every moment of every day.

Yes, he and his love were truly the greatest gift I ever received.

LETTER TO LARRY WRITTEN 7/12/19

> *My love, my Bear, my Cowboy, my Renzo, my best friend,*
>
> *Even though I am fully aware that you are gone from me and that you can never read these words, I am speaking them out loud as I write them and looking up at heaven hoping you can hear me.*
>
> *When we met, it only took me several weeks to realize that I wanted to spend the rest of my life with you. Magically you felt the same way too. You know that I proposed first that afternoon when I told you that I wanted the sanctity of a great marriage. I asked you if you were on the same page. You know what your answer was.*
>
> *July 1, 2000—what a beautiful summer day. I stood at the bottom of the circular staircase looking up at you while Michael Crawford sang "Unexpected Song," and you could tell by the look on my face that I needed you to come down the stairs to give me your love and support because my legs were shaking so much.*
>
> *You laughed about that later and asked me why I was shaking. The answer Bear was that I was so relieved to see*

*you standing there waiting for me, and I couldn't believe how fortunate I was at that moment that you loved me enough to spend your life with me.*

*You took my breath away every time you held me. You made my heart skip a beat with your smile. You always took care of me, you were always there, you never let me down in life, and I would never want you to think that in dying that I would feel that way.*

*We had Paris twice, wasn't it grand?*

*I see us standing on the first level of the Eiffel Tower in the cold winds of February looking out over the City of Lights kissing like newlyweds. We laughed that most of the people there were doing the same thing. Public displays of affection are acceptable in Paris.*

*You saw the worst side of me and loved me still. Then again, I saw some sides of you after your open-heart surgery that will remain private, I promise. Made you smile, though, didn't I?*

*When people talk about you now, they talk about how much you cared about doing things the right way. When they talk about us, they tell me how dynamic we were, how we brought laughter to their lives, how we set off our own personal fireworks that spelled out the word love.*

*Last week a friend wrote to me to say we were one giant breath of air and excitement. I would say that describes us pretty well, wouldn't you?*

*It was all as perfect as it could be until it wasn't perfect any longer.*

*You had reached your forever with me, I understand that, but accepting it is an entirely different thing.*

*There was no coming back this time. No miraculous new device that they could use to save your life. You had fought so hard with other health issues, this time your strength was gone and you had no fight left, you knew that, you gave in to it, and I know it broke your heart too.*

*I was talking to a store clerk the other day asking her to change a rewards card into my name. I went on to tell her all the hoops I had been asked to jump through over and over and how hard it was on me. She knocked the breath right out of me when she told me you are having a hard time too. I understand you want to be here still and that you know it is not possible.*

*However, if you run into Patrick Swayze you might ask him how he came back in the first movie we ever watched together. You know what I am writing about; you cried, and I cried, and I loved you more because you could show your emotional side so easily.*

*You are the love of my life, and I am proud that I was your last great love and that you chose me.*

*I miss you with every breath I take, I will love you with all my heart until I reach my forever and we are together again.*

*This is my last 143 to you dear man because 143 is no longer a working number.*

*All my love,*
*Babe*
*143*

It took me less than 4 months to write this book, and it has taken an equal amount of time to bring it to something you can hold in your hands.

I had been writing every day and posting my thoughts on social media. People suggested that I put my thoughts into a book to help others who are grieving.

There are books people can buy that do address this topic. I didn't want my book to be a "how to" manual. I wanted to share the magnificence of the love Larry and I shared, and braid into this love story suggestions of what to do throughout the process of moving forward when it happens to you because there is no if it happens to you.

Grief is the opposite of love. To deny the loss is to deny the love. It took me over 30 years to find love that encircled me with passion, security, trust, loyalty and devotion. I looked for 30 long years and when I discovered it, 20 years later I lost it, but is it truly lost?

No, it is not. I was his last great love and no one can take that away from me. My heart aches every day knowing he is gone forever, and yet my heart sings every day knowing he loved me more than life itself.

From my book:

30 years, and you see I was done, despite those who wanted to make me all undone for one night, or one week, and leave me in a crumpled mess on the floor.

# FRACTURED

My energy was gone, spent by those who did not want to stay, and just when I felt used up, the man I called a beast found me. He was captivated, mystified and intrigued, as if I was the finest wine he had ever brought to his lips and had until now, never tasted.

He got down on the floor with me. All the love he had longed for encircled him like a ring of fire, and eventually that ring of fire surrounded me, and we could see forever in each other's eyes.

Loving each other was better than anything or anyone who had come before. His forever ended, leaving me to lie on the floor where the rings of fire had once burned extinguished by my tears.

I am living, breathing proof that a fractured heart can still beat and I wrote this book to give everyone who grieves hope and faith in forever love.

*Carole L. Sanek*

I wrote this book in 2021 and because I have had the opportunity to republish it I wanted to add a postscript to you the reader telling you who and what and where I am now.

I live in Greenville, SC. I made a new life for myself away from the plethora of memories that would hit me smack in the face every day in Florida. I am still writing. I have a second book coming out soon in the form of a memoir about a significant trauma in my life. I wrote it to heal. Traumas are tough. I was traumatized when Larry died suddenly in my arms only to be kept alive by machines, until I said, "Enough is enough." We honored Larry's advanced directives.

I have a wonderful dog named Rosie. I got her from the local humane society and she is my loyal companion now. I have also made a lot of new friends, I have traveled to Europe three times focusing mainly on Italy, the trip Larry and I had planned that we never got to take.

I am still doing personal life coaching although most of my work centers on grief and I am fine with that, I know grief, well. I have a podcast seven days a week for 2-3 minutes coaching people to thrive in life, and I am going to start work soon on my third book "Why Am I Still Here?"

I hit acceptance in 2024 and realized I was falling in love with Larry all over again. This fills me with joy.

If you are grieving, know there are people who will help you, including me.

Carole L. Sanek is a certified personal life coach who has also been a ghost writer for over 10 years for clients. She has blogged and written marketing pieces for social media for others and is an award-winning blogger herself. She has won awards for her wittiness and upfront style with her diagnosis of breast can-cer years ago. When the sudden death of her beloved husband happened, those who follow her encouraged her to write a book about her grief. Carole did not want to write a "how-to" book on grieving and she chose to share their love story weaving tips and advice into each chapter.

## CONTACT INFORMATION:

My email address is carolelynnsanek@gmail.com

My website is https://carolesanek.com

My podcast is https://thrivelive.podbean.com/

www.ingramcontent.com/pod-product-compliance
Lightning Source LLC
Chambersburg PA
CBHW071452070526
44578CB00001B/315